THIS IS ME,
JACK VANCE!

(Or, More Properly, This is "I")

THIS IS ME,
JACK
VANCE!

(Or, More Properly, This is "I")

JACK VANCE

SUBTERRANEAN PRESS 2009

Second Printing

ISBN
978-1-59606-245-0

Subterranean Press
PO Box 190106
Burton, MI 48519

www.subterraneanpress.com

Motto for a Doghouse by Arthur Guiterman, page 157, reprinted with the
permission of Richard E. Sclove.
"Darkling: A Threnody by L. Bassington Mulliner" and "Good Gnus" are
reprinted by the estate of P. G. Wodehouse. All rights reserved.

In Memoriam
NORMA VANCE
(1927–2008)

Charm'd magic casements, opening on the foam
Of perilous seas, in faery lands forlorn.
—KEATS

~2222~
PRELIMINARY REMARKS

I USE THE above heading because other more usual designations seem rather too formal, and would indicate a literary structure which I doubt will be anywhere evident in the following. In the preparation of this memoir I have attempted a new and unfamiliar form of communication: namely dictation, which I find unpredictable and which calls for its own unique species of discipline. All the material in this book was recorded to tape, then transcribed by my friend Jeremy Cavaterra.

This autobiographical sketch is perhaps more of a landscape than a self-portrait—or at least a ramble across the landscape that has been my life. I recognize that my reputation, such as it is, derives from literary production; however, writing has not been the sole function of my life and I am bound to report that this book offers little on the subject in the way of shop-talk. Like any craft, writing is mastered by practice and patience, and if one has any "knack" for it at all, that very knack—paradoxically—can explicate everything under the sun but itself.

However, many remarkable persons have wandered in and out of my life, and I have been fortunate enough to live through what is certainly an interesting and eventful epoch. I have attempted to detail these persons and events, while at the same time perhaps conveying something of my attitudes toward life. The latter I have not done vehemently, nor even consciously; such is merely the inevitable by-product of telling one's own story.

On we rode, the others and I,
Over the mountains blue, and by
The Silver River, the sounding sea,
And the robber woods of Tartary.
—ROBERT LOUIS STEVENSON

CHAPTER 1

I WAS BORN in San Francisco, in the district known as Pacific Heights, halfway up the hills along the northern side of the city overlooking the bay. At this time—the year was 1916—San Francisco was known everywhere for its grace, charm, dignity, and for its beautiful prospects, fine restaurants, even respectability.

I am the middle of five children, with two older brothers (Albert and Louis), a younger brother (David) and sister (Patricia). My mother, Edith Vance (*née* Hoefler), was prominent in the social life of San Francisco. She attended the exclusive Miss Hamlin School, along with Lurline Matson of the Matson shipping lines. When she and my father were married they held a grand reception in the Fairmont Hotel, and the society section of the *Chronicle* devoted an entire page to the event. My mother was happy-go-lucky, good-natured, generous, and all my life I have not only loved her but admired and respected her.

During these early years I saw very little of my father, who was stationed in France, connected with the Red Cross in some capacity. On the other hand, I saw a great deal of my maternal grandfather, Ludwig Matthias Hoefler. He lived across the city in a splendid old Victorian mansion equipped with a wine cellar, a billiard room, and a dining room paneled in rosewood. He was a successful lawyer, a dabbler in politics, and evidently prominent in city affairs. I marvel to this day when I think of the streetcars grinding up the Haight Street hill, loaded with people on their way home from work, stopping halfway up the hill in front of my grandfather's house to let him off before proceeding up to Laguna Street.

In 1920 or '21—I don't remember the exact date—my grandfather was sent over to Germany as part of the Dawes Committee, the function of which was to improve the German economic situation. While he was abroad he visited Rome, where he saw a pair of massive marble statues representing ancient Greek pugilists. He was so taken by these statues that he ordered copies made, and these he shipped back to San Francisco as a gift to the Olympic Club, of which he was vice president. There they stand to this day, on Post Street in front of the Olympic Club.

My family lived in San Francisco until I was five years old, and I remember many episodes of these early years. One night up in the bedroom I shared with my two older brothers there was a big moth fluttering around the ceiling, and it terrified me. I remember my older brothers jumping around from bed to bed, bravely trying to capture the moth, which to my relief they finally did.

We had a cook named Alice McKittrick, whom I loved very much. One day I declared to her, who knows why, that I would like some creamed onions. So Alice cooked me some lovely creamed onions. I can still see them, as I looked down at my tray in front of me, waving my spoon over the top of them. Ultimately I decided that I really didn't want them after all. Alice watched me with pure Irish scorn on her face.

My brother David is interested in the genealogy of our family, and has acquired considerable information in this field.

In the lowlands of Scotland, Wigtownshire to be precise, there is a castle now inhabited by a gentleman about whom I know nothing except that he has done much research in regard to the Vance ancestry. His findings indicate that a pair of Norman brothers by the name of de Vaux came over with William the Conqueror in 1066. They settled in the north of England; later a cadet branch moved on into Scotland. In 1745 they espoused the wrong side of the Jacobite Rebellion and fled to Ireland, so that the family became Scotch-Irish. The Wigtown gentleman traces the family further back to Aquitaine, to nobility even, and ultimately to a Gallo-Roman family called de Vallibus. This all sounds a bit far-fetched, but when I come to think about it, all names must originate somewhere, and there is no real reason for skepticism. The name Vance, like every other, evolved from some source in antiquity—why not from de Vallibus?

I have learned that I am also descended from William Clark of the Lewis & Clark expedition. Up in Montana, so the story goes, Clark got in bed with an Indian lady, who subsequently gave birth to a boy. It was the custom of this tribe to name the child after the first thing the mother saw upon waking. The first thing she saw was a stocking, so the boy was called Stocking Clark. In due course, after a generation or two, one of Stocking Clark's descendents married into a certain Case family, which later owned a drugstore in Copperopolis, a town in the middle of California. (Oddly enough, Copperopolis figures in my own life story, but more on that later.) Case enters on my grandmother's family, giving me a streak of indigenous blood lurking around somewhere. Such, as far as I know, are my antecedents.

When I was five I started kindergarten, and there I performed a disgraceful act. In front of me sat a little girl, dark-haired and wearing a pretty green dress. For no particular reason, I picked up a pair of scissors and began cutting triangles out of the fabric of her dress. I cut away four or five such triangles before the girl noticed what I was doing. She wasn't alarmed, just rather puzzled, wondering what I had in mind. Of course there was a great hullabaloo, and my mother in shame offered to buy another dress for this little girl; but her mother said, "Oh no, don't worry about it, it's just childhood foolishness." Some of my detractors have tried to imply that this was an indication of what might be my later predilections, but this I stoutly deny. Never again have I used scissors to cut at a girl's dress!

Fifty miles east of San Francisco is the delta region, where three rivers—the Sacramento, the San Joaquin, and the Mokelumne—come together. They are intersected by dozens of inlets called *sloughs*, which create numerous islands. The word "slough" is something of a misnomer, since these waterways are extremely picturesque, with weeping willows and cottonwoods along the banks. In 1921, my grandfather acquired a property alongside one of these waterways, known as Little Dutch Slough. On the north side of this property was a dairy—with a barn, a shed, all the equipment, and lots of cows—which my grandfather leased out. Across the fields, about half a mile away, was another house, which my grandfather used as a weekend retreat. This was Green Lodge Ranch, a rambling old house surrounded by locust and pepper trees, with a water tower beside it supporting a tank.

In the summer of 1922 it was decided that the family—my mother and we five kids—should move up to Green Lodge Ranch and spend the summer there. This met with our approval, since there was a barn on the premises, housing a little Shetland pony, another horse, and an old-fashioned buggy. There was even a well on the property, but the pump was out of commission, and so for a while we had to hitch up the horse and buggy, drive to our neighbors' about a mile away, fill up some barrels with water and drive back to the ranch. This went on for several months until we finally restored the well to working order and filled the tank, which made things a lot more convenient.

So far I haven't mentioned my aunt, Nellie Holbrook. Our house in San Francisco was 2660 Filbert Street, and she lived at 2664 Filbert Street, next door. Aunt Nellie was prim and prudish, to the degree that whenever I would play one of my records, she refused to use the word "jazz," but instead referred to the music as "zazz." I won't go into further detail with regard to her, except to say that over the years, she caused my mother a great deal of trouble. She was my father's sister, and had an almost unnatural devotion to him; she was wildly jealous of my mother. While we were up at Green Lodge Ranch, she took occasion to rent our house to some people who paid a very handsome rent. At the end of the summer, when we had been scheduled to move back to the city, my aunt urged us to stay where we were. It was very healthy for us children up at the ranch, she said, so why not stay put? The family would profit, she went on, by renting the house, and we children could go to school there and lead a wholesome country life. My mother, under pressure from my father, finally agreed to this situation.

About half a mile east of Green Lodge Ranch was a quaint old-fashioned two-room school, The Iron House School. It must have been at least fifty years old at the time. I started first grade there, and my brothers and sister took up their appropriate grades.

When I was in second grade, the teacher Miss Lawson formed a harmonica club. She taught us all how to play Marine Band harmonicas, which at the time cost 50¢. I still play the harmonica, thanks to Miss Lawson.

During these times my father resided at Green Lodge Ranch only occasionally, and was just more often elsewhere, on business ventures or in San Francisco at my aunt's house. This did not bother us kids too much, because he was a rather bluff, boisterous, self-righteous chap, and, if I must say so, a bit of a bully. When my two older brothers graduated from Iron House, my father and my aunt persuaded them into moving to San Francisco to go to high school, where, so my aunt was convinced, they would enjoy social advantages unavailable in their rural environment. My mother disapproved strongly, but she was outvoted by my two brothers, my father and my aunt, and so the household became further divided.

As for me, I didn't care much one way or the other. At the time, I was a weedy young fellow, rather bookish, with short dark hair, glasses—my eyes even in those days were bad—and not particularly gregarious. My grandfather used to call me Steinmetz, which did not please me especially, since Steinmetz was no Tom Mix or Douglas Fairbanks.

My grandfather used to drive up from the city every weekend, in a beautiful Twin Six Packard Saloon. He himself could not drive, so the car was driven by George Slade, his chauffeur. George had his quarters on the top floor of the house on Haight Street, where during his off-hours he could be heard practicing the saxophone.

Every Friday my brother David, my sister Pat and I were supposed to tidy up the front yard: rake it, make sure there weren't any leaves in the driveway, and generally make the place look spruce. About three-o'-clock in the afternoon we would start looking up and down the road. Pretty soon we would see the Packard come trundling down, and with excitement, because out of the car would come first of all my grandfather, followed by his mother my great-grandmother, then my grandmother, and often guests that he would bring up to spend the weekend at the ranch. His guests were of all descriptions: sometimes a little flaky, sometimes business people. Regardless, we always enjoyed these weekends. On Saturday mornings, my grandmother and my mother would chop up kidneys for the kidney sauté; that was our usual Saturday breakfast. Sunday dinner was a three- or four-rib roast beef, or occasionally roast lamb or pork, but always a noteworthy occasion, after which my grandfather and his family and guests would climb aboard the Packard and return to San Francisco, and my mother would sigh with relief. Then life would proceed quietly until the next Friday afternoon, when it all began again.

On his trips to the country my grandfather was accustomed to stop by Johnny Heinhold's saloon in Oakland, in what is now Jack London Square. Heinhold knew Jack London, and although this was the time of Prohibition, he and my grandfather would quietly enjoy a few belts of contraband. Then my grandfather would drive to the Hunt Hatch warehouse, in which he had a partial interest, and there would load the Packard with sacks of oranges, apples or other fruit, and bring these to the ranch.

I spent a very pleasant childhood, naturally with its ups and downs. The window of my bedroom commanded a beautiful view to the west, and it was especially beautiful at dusk. Far, far, far to the north, I could see the Coast Range starting up, which as it came down to the south got larger and larger and culminated in Mt. Diablo before dwindling away into the far, far south, so that you had to turn your head to take it all in. Every evening about the middle of dusk the Santa Fe train went past about two miles west, and whistled at the crossing—*"Woo-wooooo, woo-wooooo!"*—the most lonesome sound there is. It affects me even now as I remember it.

These were pleasant years, and I had much to keep me occupied. I rode the pony all around the countryside, and in summertime we would swim almost every day at the swimming hole. There was also a rowboat which we were privileged to use; on occasion we would take it out onto the beautiful sloughs among the islands and along the levees where the willows and cottonwoods grew. Occasionally, on the weekends, and at my grandfather's instigation, the whole family would go out mushroom-hunting. We would range the nearby fields and would seldom fail to come home with a basketful. During one of these mushroom hunts one of my grandfather's cronies, Adolph Schroeder, discovered an enormous mushroom measuring a foot across the cap. His find made the papers in San Francisco.

I became interested in kite-flying, and I used to make all manner of kites: box kites, airplane kites, plain old-fashioned diamond-shaped kites. I'd take these out into the alfalfa fields adjacent to our house, lie down and fly them. All afternoon, lying in the fragrant alfalfa, I'd watch my kite move across the sky.

Around this time I also took up stiltwalking. I started very modestly, on six-inch stilts, then grew bolder and went up to a foot, then two feet, and finally to the extreme of eight-foot stilts, which I could only mount by climbing a tree and getting aboard from there. As anyone who has walked on stilts knows, it's not all that difficult as long as the stilts are kept moving.

The house at Green Lodge Ranch was full of books, which my mother had brought up with her from San Francisco. My mother had catholic tastes, and among these books were fantasy novels by Robert W. Chambers, such as *Tracer of Lost Persons*, *The King in Yellow*, *Maker of the Moons*. There were also works by Edgar Rice Burroughs. My mother described how, about 1915 in the magazine *Blue Book*, there appeared the first installment of a serial called *Tarzan of the Apes*. She said that this story instantly had become a fad among all of her acquaintances. So at the ranch, we had not only *Tarzan of the Apes*, but also *The Son of Tarzan* and other Burroughs books, including the *Barsoom* books—*John Carter of Mars*, *Princess of Mars*, *Warlord of Mars*— all of which I read and reread. We also had all the *Oz* books by L. Frank Baum, as well as several series of boys' books, emanating from the Edward Stratemeyer fiction factory: *Motor Boys*, *Dave Porter*, *Tom Swift*, and the *Roy Rockwood* books—which I now perceive to be precursors of modern science fiction.

About three miles west of us was the town of Oakley. In the drugstore was a magazine rack, and there I came upon the *Amazing Stories* quarterly, edited by Hugo Gernsback, and also the *Amazing Stories* monthly. I subsequently discovered *Weird Tales* and subscribed to it. It was a banner day of the month when I ran down to the mailbox in front of Iron House School to find it there. Of the authors I read in *Weird Tales* I recall the names Seabury Quinn, H. P. Lovecraft, C. L. Moore, and one which I assumed to be a pseudonym: Nictzin Dyalhis. I was amused to think that this chap had gone to such pains to give himself a memorable identity. Later I learned that this had been his real name! His father, a Welshman, had been obsessed by the Aztecs, and so had given him the name Nictzin.

Another resource was the public library in Oakley, where I read anything that seemed interesting.

The years went past, these golden years of the '20s. At Iron House School I had no friends to speak of; in fact I was thought to be rather eccentric. But I was not overly concerned. One afternoon, two girls came up to me. These were the prettiest girls in the school: one dark, the other blonde. They cornered me, menacingly, and said: "We hear you've been talking about us." I said no, I had not. They said, "Yes! You said that when you grow up you're going to have one of us for a wife and the other for a girlfriend. And we can tell you—you'd better change your mind!"

"No, no, no!" I said. "I never said any such thing."

"Don't try to fool us," they said, "this is definitely what we heard."

For a fact, at that stage in my life, I entertained no such thoughts.

At the ranch we had many visitors, some of whom were down on their luck. There was Jack Blossom, the golf pro, currently employed in laying out miniature golf courses. Another was Eddie Carroll, who had something to do with baseball, and who was also a chemist; he had invented a method for detecting how much water there was at the bottom of an oil tank. Others came from dubious backgrounds. There was a pair of gentlemen whose occupation was selling Tsarist Russian bonds to investors who were innocent enough to believe that Stalin was anxious to redeem old Romanoff securities. But the most important, as far as I was concerned, and the one who had the greatest influence on me, was George Gould, a pianist of remarkable abilities. My mother was also a good pianist; she could sight-read but could not improvise. George played music which utterly captivated me: he played jazz, as I was to learn. At one time, George Gould's orchestra was the best in San Francisco, better than Paul Whiteman's or Art Hickman's.[1]

A mile south of the ranch was a town called Knightsen. At the farm center every Friday night there would be a whist party followed by dancing. My mother would play piano for this dancing, sometimes with a saxophone and drum, but just as often alone. When George was with us, she would take him up there to play the piano, and it was wonderful to see the dancers respond to the way he swung that music. George at this time was past his first youth, and clearly not in good health. He left the ranch to take a job at Stockton, and several months later we learned that he had died there.

Along about this time, I read a book by Sir James Jeans, *The Universe Around Us*. I became involved with a new preoccupation: namely, identifying the stars. I obtained star charts. I would take a flashlight, cover it over with a red bandana, lie out in the sand a few hundred feet from the house, stare up into the sky and trace out the constellations. In due course I learned all the constellations and all the first magnitude stars, and many of the second magnitude stars. I find it hard to convey how much

---

1. When the British royal family came to San Francisco, they stayed at the Palace Hotel, where the ballroom was known as The Rose Room. Hickman wrote a tune to commemorate this royal visit, *Rose Room*, which is still a standard.

pleasure this pursuit gave me. The stars all became familiar, friends almost, and I rejoiced when, in the middle of the summer, Fomalhaut would appear over the southern horizon. Even now, as I write this, I can envision how the skies looked, aglow with those wonderful stars: Arcturus, Vega, Betelgeuse, Antares, Sirius, Achernar, Algol, Polaris.

During these years, my father was not much in evidence. He had acquired a hacienda of three thousand acres near Tepic, in Mexico, not far from Puerto Vallarta. He left San Francisco and went to live on this hacienda, where he remained, and we saw no more of him. In effect my mother and father were separated, although the divorce did not occur until some years later.

We still received income from the rental of our house in San Francisco, but my aunt managed to keep this to a minimum, so that we were obliged to rely upon the largesse of my grandfather, who himself was encountering financial difficulties. Breweries were his principal clients, but with the coming of Prohibition the breweries declined, and so correspondingly did my grandfather's income.

In 1928 I was graduated from Iron House and started high school. I was then eleven years old. I was small and thin, without any social graces. As a consequence I was not particularly popular; the girls never looked twice at me.

This was about the time that my aunt convinced my two older brothers that life in San Francisco was far more exciting than life at the ranch, and far more sophisticated. She lured them away to live with her in San Francisco and so split up the family. My mother was left at the ranch with her three younger children: myself, Patricia and David.

My grandfather continued to be on hand on weekends, with all the usual excitement. He liked to rise early in the morning, and would take himself into the kitchen, make himself coffee, pour the coffee into a mug, followed by cream from a pitcher.

One morning he poured himself a second cup of coffee, then cream—and along with the cream came a dead mouse, which plopped into the cup.

My grandfather was not a man to stifle his emotions, and on this occasion the remarks were loud and profane.

I recall my grandfather's favorite imprecation, which predictably came in response to some mischief or misfortune. He spoke always with dramatic fervor, in a measured and staccato style, using a rasping, almost lyrical cadence: "God damn the world, by quarter-sections!"

When my brother Louis departed for San Francisco he left behind a bright orange Model T Ford Roadster, which he sold to me for $5. I had no driving license, but still I drove this Model T around the countryside without remorse.

This Model T figures in many of my adventures. On one occasion I took it to the high school baseball diamond, and there met my friend Lewis Berry, who drove a Model T of his own. We drove back and forth, circled, slid, stirred up a lot of dust, and left the diamond in a sorry state indeed. On the following Monday, Lewis and I were summoned to the principal's office, where he gave us what-for, and sent us out to rake the baseball diamond until it was smooth as a billiard table. Lewis and I toiled in the heat for several hours until the job was done.

One night I had a flat tire, and while I was fixing it, I stood in front of the tail light. A car came up behind and tossed me into a ditch. Luckily the car was being driven very slowly by an old Italian farm worker. Still, I can't imagine how I escaped that collision without broken bones.

The Model T also provided a more amusing function of which I am not particularly proud. I attached a spark coil and a chain which, when lowered, provided a ground. When I touched a button, anyone standing with their hands on the car would receive the most amusing jolt of high-voltage electricity. On one occasion, this ploy backfired. I had raised the hood and was working on the motor when my brother David pressed the button and I jumped six feet in the air. While he sat grinning, I realized that the ploy no longer amused me.

One morning David and I, with a boy named Wendell Pond, drove to the base of Mt. Diablo, where we parked the Model T and climbed to the summit of the south peak. Then we returned to the car and started to drive home. Along the way the transmission developed some alarming grinding noises and we were barely able to limp back to Green Lodge Ranch. My grandfather refused to finance repairs, stating that he had already put too much money into the wretched vehicle, so it was rolled into the barn to await a time when funds became available. Such time never came, and the Model T languished in the barn and I drove it no more.

At school, one year followed another. I played a great deal of tennis, and spent much of my time in the science laboratory. Sometimes I tried to formulate substances of my own contrivance, hoping to hit upon some interesting chemical reaction. Luckily I failed, since the science teacher had the forethought to include no fuming nitric acid among the chemicals available to the students.

As the years passed, I gradually came to realize that the girls no longer regarded me as a pariah, and even, so I was told, thought me rather engaging. I developed a crush upon a pretty girl named Helen Ricks, who occasionally consented to accompany me on romantic drives through the moonlight. In the senior yearbook, members of the graduating class were listed along with their foibles. There it was reported that my favorite remark was: "Do you want to go for a ride, Helen?"

My high school was not large, and there were only thirty-eight students in the graduating class. Many of these went on to live lives which, at the time of graduation, we would have considered unpredictable and astonishing, if not worse. Richard Townsley almost immediately was stricken by some rare disease and died. Two of the group committed suicide: one was Jimmy Cooper, a casual young scapegrace with an impenetrable personality. He was thin, sandy-haired, nonchalant, and he took no interest whatever in school activities. He was also seen smoking cigarettes, which at the time was not fashionable. The other was Nola Frye, a strikingly beautiful girl, who was also very proper and even prim. I remember an occasion when she was playing tennis, while my friend Henry White and I were sitting on a bench nearby. Henry, who was usually restrained in his conduct, now was prompted to call out: "Nola, by golly but you've got a beautiful figure!"

Nola, flustered and blushing, swung around and regarded Henry with disapproval. "Henry, you shouldn't say such things," she told him. A year or two after graduation, she killed herself, and no one knows why, although there were rumors of an unhappy love affair.

Kyla Moore married a jockey who was later sent to jail on grounds of doping racehorses. Another girl, whose name I won't mention, by rumor had taken herself to Reno, where she engaged in a rather scandalous profession.

The strangest of all was what happened to Henry White. Henry, in addition to being my best friend at the time, was a good-natured, lanky chap; his hair was so blond as to be almost white, and he carried himself with a jaunty swagger. He was universally popular. After high school, I lost track of him for several years, during which time he married a girl with extravagant tastes, who later divorced him.

I next came upon Henry almost by accident. We brought each other up to date as to what was going on in our lives. He mentioned that he'd been divorced, but said that at the moment, his ex-wife had gone off on a trip somewhere, and that he'd undertaken to look after her dogs. She had eight miniature French poodles. Henry was supposed to go to her house every day to feed and water them, groom them, and comb their fur. A week went by, and I failed to hear from Henry. Then the news came: Henry had been found murdered in the driveway of his ex-wife's house. All eight of the poodles had also been killed; four were arranged along one side of his body, and four on the other side. The perpetrator remained unknown.

As for me, my life had slanted off in a different direction. During my last year of high school, I became friendly with one Glen Douglas. This was the year 1932, the heart of the Great Depression. Glen and his family were among the migrants who had come out in great numbers from Oklahoma, Kansas, Texas and elsewhere. Glen was intelligent and easy to get along with. He and I used to discuss cosmology, philosophy, and the way the world goes, at great length. After graduation he planned to attend junior college in Porterville, a town far to the south, half under the first rise of the Sierra Nevada and surrounded by orange groves. I had no hopes of immediately starting university, and so I became intrigued with Glen's program.

In the fall, we set off to the south. We traveled by hitchhiking and riding the Santa Fe boxcars. The Santa Fe was easy in this respect, and allowed hobos and bums to ride box cars without too much trouble. Southern Pacific, however, was very strict, and the railroad bulls were not at all kind to this sort of passenger. Nevertheless, we arrived in Porterville, rented a cabin among several other such cabins in a compound where agricultural workers lived, and started at junior college. We had very little money, and were forced to live in spartan style. We ate a lot of beans, and a dish called "slumgullion." This is actually quite good: it consists of canned corned beef, shredded and fried to a frizzle, hashed potatoes, and lots of onions, all browned together in a skillet. It's a lot better than it sounds, I assure you.

The atmosphere at junior college was totally different from that of high school. I found it to be somewhat formal, impersonal, even class-conscious, and the students tended to divide into cliques. None of this, however, affected me or Glen, who were off in a group of our own—namely the two of us.

I made several new friends, and became infatuated with a girl named Alice Wood. She was tall, dark-haired, and unutterably beautiful. She took no heed whatever of me, and I doubt if she was even aware of my existence. In biology class, I noticed that if I looked into the microscope, and adjusted the mirror in a certain way, I could see her at her desk. I spent most of the class period staring at her through the eyepiece of the microscope. Glen became aware of my preoccupation, and jeered at me mercilessly.

In general, despite our enforced propinquity, Glen and I got along quite well. Only a single trivial aspect of our shared existence served to irritate each of us, in varying degrees. Glen had brought a guitar with him, which he was learning to play. He had found the chords for "Red River Valley" and one or two other such tunes. He was trying to learn a more complicated song, currently very popular, whose name I can't now recall. He played and sang this song with great diligence, but every time he reached a certain sequence, he played a note incorrectly, flatting it, so that the tune sounded off-key. I politely tried to correct him, but he paid no heed, and the next time he played the tune, he'd play the same off-note again. So once more I would correct him, which I could see annoyed him, and eventually I discontinued my advice.

This was about the only time we got on each other's nerves. Glen was really a fine fellow: decent, generous, good-natured, and he loved to discuss abstruse topics, although he had no interest in science or mathematics. I recall a time while we were still in high school when he told me that he had invented a revolutionary device which was certain to make him a great deal of money. He did not like to talk about it for fear that the news would leak out before he had secured the patent. Still, he agreed to describe this marvelous concept to me on the basis of absolute confidentiality, to which I agreed.

Glen proceeded to describe his invention. The basis was a cigar-shaped balloon about twenty feet long or so, filled with buoyant gas, and outfitted with a hammock-like device attached below. In this hammock a farm worker could lie face-down while he drifted slowly over the field picking peas, tomatoes and other produce. This device, so Glen assured me, would greatly facilitate the work and also minimize the aches and pains attendant upon such an occupation. I listened politely, but made no comment, except to reassure Glen that I would maintain total secrecy with regard to his plans.

My funds, meanwhile, were growing short, to the point of disappearing. I wrote to my grandfather, asking for some help, but I received no answer, which puzzled me. Finally, I ran out of funds totally. I was forced to quit junior college. I took myself home to the ranch—hitchhiking, riding boxcars, and finally arriving late one afternoon—only to find the place deserted. No one was home: not my mother, nor my brother, nor sister, nor any indication as to their whereabouts. I telephoned San Francisco, and learned that my grandfather had died during the previous week. My mother had discovered that he too was utterly broke, which explained why he had sent me no money at Porterville.

Many years later, I chanced to encounter Glen Douglas one last time. The occasion was a school reunion. He invited me and my wife Norma to visit him at his house in Covelo, a town near an Indian reservation. We accepted, and a week later set off to the north.

We discovered that Glen had established himself on a hilltop in a forest of tall pines and firs. His house was quaint and picturesque; he had built it himself to his own specifications, acting upon the influence of his memories of growing up in Oklahoma.

On the evening of our visit, Glen informed us that he had bought into the business of selling and renting forklifts, at which he had prospered to such a degree that he was now retired. Whenever the mood came upon him, or when he felt like picking up some spare change, he would drive down into the Indian reservation and play poker with the Indians, always returning with $50 or $60.

In the morning Norma and I took our farewell. We invited Glen and his wife Ruby to visit us at our home in Oakland. But they never showed up, and I never saw Glen again.

I cannot stand where once I stood;
It takes a life to learn
That none may steer a course to shear
The trail of light astern.
—S. FOWLER WRIGHT

CHAPTER 2

I MENTIONED THAT my mother and father had divorced, but perhaps I did not go into all the attendant detail. The facts were that before my mother and father were married, my father had transferred title to the house on Filbert Street to my aunt. This was a secret, so that at the time of the divorce, my mother thought that the house was a joint property. She was disabused. In short, she had been swindled by my aunt and my father. When the divorce became final, my aunt stopped making over any income proceeding from rental of the house, so that when my grandfather died, we were left without any income whatever. Green Lodge Ranch was still under mortgage, and the bank, receiving no payments, foreclosed.

My mother went to work. She took several jobs, of varying degrees of dignity, and I must say that in retrospect I admire her tremendously. She was always good-humored, good-natured, she lost neither her spirits nor her temper, as many other ladies in her circumstances might have done. I also went to work, as a farmhand at the nearby Burroughs Bros. Dairy, though the pay was not very good.

We moved to a rented house in Oakley. During fruit season, I picked apricots at 20¢ an hour, and later cherries—at 1¢ a pound!

So the summer passed. In the autumn, my uncle telephoned me from San Francisco. This was Charles Holbrook, from whom I derive my middle name, a man I liked very much—almost as much as I detested my aunt. He could best be described as having been a promoter, concerned mainly with oil and mining prospects. His income fluctuated according to circumstances; sometimes he was very prosperous, sometimes down on his luck. During the '20s, his fortunes were at the flood, and he always kept $50,000 in the bank, which he regarded as a sheet anchor. Every morning, he came down to breakfast and turned to the stock reports, where he had been following the fortunes of a stock called "Black Sulfur." Every day he'd utter some comment, such as, "Up again! I should have gotten into this before." And the next day he would again cry out, "Ah! Black Sulfur! It's going to hit a new high." This went on.

In 1929 the great crash occurred. When my uncle read the stock pages, he shook his head sadly, and told my aunt, "Luckily, I didn't have any dealings with Black Sulfur—it's gone down to practically zero. But that doesn't affect us too much; we still have our nest egg, the $50,000, and before long, we'll be back on our feet, since I've got some new prospects."

At this my aunt looked at him with a sick expression. She said, "Charlie, I've got something to confess."

"Oh?" said my uncle. "What's that?"

"Well, I became so engaged by your talk of Black Sulfur that I took that $50,000 and invested it in Black Sulfur stock."

My uncle uttered a terrible cry, and nearly fell out of his chair.

One day, my uncle telephoned me to the effect that certain of his associates had taken a lease on an old hydraulic mine that had been closed down for a lack of water. This was the True Grit Mine, located just east of Camptonville, a little town deep in the Sierra Nevada mountains. They hoped to bring it back into operation.

The first stage of the program was to bring water from various sources around the mountains to the mine, where it would be projected under pressure against the gold-bearing sediments. The resultant slurry would flow over riffles, where the gold would be collected.

In charge of the project was Roy Laylander, who was something short of middle age, thin and sinewy, with sparse long hair and a suspicious disposition. No one liked him very much. Also on hand was a bulldozer operator, a cook, and a labor force, which consisted of my brother Louis, Laylander's son Paul, Henry Morrison, who was about my age, and me.

I must also mention Charlie Donnelly, who was not part of the working crew, but who for several years had lived alone at the True Grit Mine functioning as caretaker. Charlie must have been about sixty years old. Previously, he had worked in San Francisco as a cartoonist for the *San Francisco Chronicle*, where he had become almost a celebrity. His work was vastly amusing until his reliance upon a liquid consisting largely of ethanol brought an end to his career. My uncle and some of his other friends established Charlie at the mine as a caretaker, and there, perhaps due to his isolation, he dried out.

I became fond of Charlie. He was a wonderfully funny man, and commanded an inexhaustible repertory of poems, limericks, impersonations and other material, most of it naughty, some not so naughty—for instance, that epic ballad known as "Ivan Skavinsky Skavar." One of his productions simulated what would seem to be a stage show or circus act; each segment ended with the command, "Willie, turn the crank!"

I also learned from Charlie the song "The Big Black Bull Come Down from the Mountains," and a rollicking composition known as "Christopher Colombo." This is decidedly naughty, in parts at least, but I can't resist the temptation to include a few of the verses. I hope no one will be offended.

The work starts off with a description of Colombo:

He knew the world was round-O
His balls hung to the ground-O
That fornicatin', family-breakin'
Rattle-ass scamp Colombo!

The next verses tell how he goes to the queen of Spain to ask for ships and cargo, and then sets off across the Atlantic, until his men, due to lack of female companionship, almost become frantic. At last, after forty days and forty nights, he sights an island. He approaches, drops anchor, and then—

Upon the shore there stood a whore;
They stripped off shirts and collars.
In twenty minutes by the clock
She'd made a thousand dollars.
Those were the days of no clap cure;
The doctors were not many.
The only doc that he could find
Was a sad old quack named Benny.
Colombo strode up to the doc,
His smile serene and placid;
The goddamn' doc burned off his cock
With hydrochloric acid!

Enough of Charlie Donnelly and his witticisms. Louis, Paul, Henry and I worked clearing manzanita, digging ditches, building wooden troughs, all intended to bring water down to the mine.

On our first payday, I became aware of an inequity which I found irritating. I learned that while Henry and I were being paid $2.50 a day, Laylander's son Paul and my brother Louis were being paid $5 a day. I complained to Laylander and told him that Henry and I were producing as much work as was Paul. Laylander responded in a cold voice that he had assessed the situation, and that the pay scale would remain as it was.

Henry and I were displeased. We surmised that Laylander had spoken to Paul, because now Paul was working like crazy, running when he could have walked, sweat pouring off his face.

A day or so later, Henry and I were working in the forest cleaning out a ditch. We were discussing the current circumstances; neither of us was happy. I cried out, "I don't blame Paul, but that Laylander is a real son of a bitch!" About this time I chanced to look over my shoulder, and there, about ten feet away, stood Laylander himself. He looked me over a minute or two, then turned and walked away.

Weeks passed, and nothing much happened, but a sinister pressure seemed to hang in the air. My birthday was coming up, and I decided to take a weekend off in order to celebrate with my family. On Friday evening I drove south. The usual festivities occurred; I spent a pleasant weekend. Sunday afternoon, I was preparing to drive north again when I received a telephone call. Laylander was on the line, and he notified me that my employment had been terminated. I was out of a job.

My mother, with David and Patricia, still occupied the rented house on the outskirts of Oakley. I stayed there for a short period, trying without success to find employment. We were living through the very depths of the Depression, and jobs were as scarce as hen's teeth. Finally, in desperation, I went to stay with my aunt in San Francisco, and there, through the influence of one of my grandfather's friends, I was offered a job at the Olympic Club.

There was no prestige attached to this job. I wore a monkey suit, and functioned as a bellhop and elevator operator. The pay was low and working conditions were wretched. Nevertheless,

I clung to this job for about a year, a time I now recall as perhaps the most abysmal of my entire life.

I was living with my aunt at her house on Filbert Street. In my spare time, I had already started to write. I wrote some poetry, and some rudimentary science fiction stories.

At one of my aunt's dinner parties, she entertained Stanton Coblentz, editor of the *Wings Quarterly* magazine, which was devoted to poetry. Coblentz also wrote science fiction stories which were published in various magazines of the time. My aunt insisted that I show him my productions, but Coblentz did not think very highly either of my poetry or my stories.

My aunt wanted me to work around the house during my off-hours. But I had far better things to do with my time than wash woodwork. I quarreled with my aunt and moved out to a rooming house across the city operated by my grandfather's old cook, where the atmosphere was much easier, although I missed playing cribbage with my uncle during the evenings.

During this period I became ever more indoctrinated into that wonderful music known as jazz, and here I do not refer to that field known as "new jazz" which, in my opinion, bears the same relationship to the true jazz as the Cubists bear to Botticelli.

The first record I ever bought was Duke Ellington's *Daybreak Express*, which I still regard as a masterpiece. At an overstocked outlet on Market Street named "Zack," I found records being sold for 5¢ apiece, and I picked up a number of records which subsequently would become collectors' items. On the radio, a weekly program known as "The Camel Caravan" was broadcast every Thursday night, featuring the great Casa Loma Orchestra, which to this day, in my opinion, has never been excelled.

My salary from the Olympic Club was by no means large, but I managed to send a few dollars every month to my mother. I also invested in a 1924 Harley Davidson motorcycle, which I used to ride over the hills to Oakley on my day off to be with my family. One day it broke down; I don't know exactly how, but I was forced to leave it in Oakley and return to San Francisco by bus. When I returned two weeks later, I found that my sister's boyfriend Frank had cannibalized my vehicle, and I was forced to take it back to San Francisco in a basket. A few days later I took this corpse of a Harley to a dealer and turned it in for an Indian, lighter and less powerful than the Harley, but which turned out to be quite dependable.

All my life I have been motivated by challenges. When I see a challenge, I feel the impulse to overcome it. This is a very deep unconscious thing, probably common to most people but not always pronounced. Perhaps, in my own case, it is the need to answer the question to oneself: Are you capable of doing this thing, are you brave enough to meet this challenge?

Around 1935, while I was still working my dreadful job at the Olympic Club, the Bay Bridge was being built between San Francisco and Oakland. The first two towers of the bridge were up. One night, I went out onto the bridge and walked up the cable, high up over the water, to the top of the first tower. It was a thrilling experience. I was perfectly safe; there were handholds on each side of the cable. At the top, I got ready to swoop down and climb up to the top of the second tower. Then I heard, ahead of me, the voices of workmen. I retreated, went back home and to bed, feeling full of some sort of triumph that I had accomplished this silly, reckless, foolish feat. Yet here I reveal part of my character. Perhaps it was an inner feeling of weakness that I was trying to compensate for.

I continued to work at the Olympic Club until the manager, in a spasm of cost-cutting, reduced the labor force, and I was released.

My uncle Charles Holbrook, or Charlie, during his prosperous days had involved himself in mining deals, oil leases, and other such ventures. Charlie was a good-hearted fellow, easygoing, generous. Among his associates was Buck Finley, who had contacts everywhere, especially with Western-Knapp, a firm involved in the construction of mining mills and the like.

Through my uncle's connections with Buck Finley and Western-Knapp, I was hired to work with a surveyor as his rodman. We were sent off to survey a tract of land in the Sierra Nevada foothills.

The surveyor's name was Joe Resnick. He was about forty years old, intelligent and efficient. He would set up his transit at some convenient spot while I would struggle up and down the hillside through the manzanita, carrying stakes and graduated rods. The manzanita, if anyone is interested, is a crotchety shrub growing as high as six feet tall. The stem bends and twists; branches thrust out in all directions. The wood is extremely hard, the dark red core surrounded by a white layer. If some enterprising botanist were to manipulate the manzanita's genes inducing the stem to grow straight and tall, with a diameter of at least six inches, the result would be the most beautiful hardwood in the world.

When the survey was completed I returned to San Francisco, where I learned that Western-Knapp was starting a new job at Copperopolis, the town in the Gold Country I have previously mentioned. Through the agency of Buck Finley I went to work at Copperopolis.

There were no lodging facilities at Copperopolis, so the crew took up residence in the Calaveras Hotel at Angels Camp, a town about twelve miles east of Copperopolis. The hotel was a rambling old two-story affair, built during the nineteenth century, and rather resembled the hotels shown in Wild West movies. The amenities were at best adequate, but the rates were correspondingly moderate. When I was first shown into my room, I found that the bed had a remarkable sag in the middle. I was about to ask for another room, but I tried the bed and, to my astonishment, found it quite comfortable, and so I made no complaints.

The superintendent of the job was a middle-aged engineer named Eric Freitag, who was tough and gruff but, in the main, easy to get along with. One Sunday morning I sat in the hotel lobby reading a newspaper. The door opened and Freitag appeared, and with him his son and daughter. The boy was about eighteen, the girl about sixteen. The girl's name, so I learned later, was Dorothy. She was dark-haired, rather slim, very graceful. I thought she was the most beautiful thing I had ever seen in my life, and I fell in love with her instantly. She looked around the lobby but I don't think she noticed me. Presently they left the lobby, and I wondered if I would ever see her again.

One Saturday evening two or three weeks later, a man about thirty-five years old wearing boots, khakis and a brown jacket registered at the hotel. His name was Kelsey. Later in the evening, I entered into a conversation with him. I learned that he held a degree in geology, but now occupied himself prospecting the Gold Country, exploring sites which had not been adequately developed and had been abandoned, but which, so he explained, with new management and adequate capital might yet prove profitable. The next day, Sunday, he planned to visit such a site, which by some odd coincidence was near the town Kelseyville. He invited me to accompany him on this expedition, and I accepted.

Sunday morning, therefore, we set off, and about 10:30 arrived at the site in which Kelsey was interested. This was situated in a valley surrounded by low hills and consisted of a pasture of forty or fifty acres on which was an old farmhouse, in ruin, and an area which apparently at one time had been a pond or a small lake, but which was now an expanse of dried mud. At the center of this mud was a construction resting on a barge. There was a hopper at one end of this barge and riffles down either side. Kelsey explained that the barge, which he called a "doodlebug," was no longer in operation owing to lack of water, even though gold was everywhere accessible. To demonstrate, Kelsey brought up a pan, into which he shoveled a quantity of dirt dug at random from the pasture. He took the pan and its contents to a nearby creek. After about five minutes of sloshing water through the pan, he showed me what he had achieved: in the bottom of the pan was a quarter-cup of black iron oxide liberally flecked with gold flakes. I was impressed.

We returned to Angels Camp. The next day was Monday and I went to work. In the evening, back at the hotel, I discovered that Kelsey had departed. I never saw him again.

A month or two later the job at Copperopolis ended, and the crew was transferred to a new job just starting up near Battle Mountain, Nevada.

Battle Mountain, so we discovered, was a lonely little community almost lost in the sagebrush about fifty miles north of Winnemucca. The town clearly dated from times long past, when a number of silver mines had been in full operation. The silver lodes had in due course become exhausted, and the town gradually lapsed into somnolence.

Currently, only two establishments which showed any relevance to these olden times survived. The first was the Buckhorn Hotel, where the crew took up residence, and which still retained a few vestiges of Victorian elegance. Second, and a hundred yards north along the main street, was the Sunset Saloon, a rambling two-story structure which at one time had been painted dark brown. At the front, a door opened into the saloon proper, a dim, rather shabby chamber with a bar at one end and several card tables along with a pinball machine at the other.

THIS IS ME, JACK VANCE!

Around the side of the building another door opened into a large parlor, furnished in a style which can best be described as genteel opulence. There were several sofas, upholstered chairs, a piano, and a great deal of plush velvet which had once been maroon, purple, and dark green, but which now showed signs of wear. Around this parlor a number of ladies sat at their ease. They were of various description, and it would not be gentlemanly to guess at their ages; but all wore costumes which they evidently considered their best and most appealing. Clearly, the parlor was where the citizens of Battle Mountain came and indulged themselves in discreet recreation. In short, and to be succinct, this was the town whorehouse.

Five miles east of town, a branch of the old silver lode had been discovered, and here Western-Knapp was constructing a mining mill. My work was familiar; I dug with pick and shovel, mixed concrete, unloaded trucks, wheeled concrete in the barrow from a mixer to where it would be dumped into the forms. The main novelty was that while Copperopolis had been hot, Battle Mountain was cold.

One of the carpenters, Robby Hicks, was a rather unusual character. He was about thirty-five, tall, lanky, assertive, blond, blue-eyed, sun-tanned, lantern-jawed. During a period of damp weather, Hicks came down with a cold. He dosed himself with pills, syrups, tinctures, herbal tea, nose drops, all to no avail. The cold persisted.

Hicks was not a patient man, and one night he declared that he would cure himself using a remedy dictated by certain precepts of folk medicine, and furthermore he would undertake the cure on this very evening. He consulted his friends; two of the carpenters agreed to participate in the venture. I, out of sheer curiosity, joined the group.

We proceeded to the Sunset Saloon. Using the side door, we entered the parlor, where we received a flattering welcome from the ladies. After a time, Hicks and his two friends mounted the stairway, each accompanied by one of the ladies. I took refuge in a corner of a sofa and made myself as inconspicuous as possible. The ladies, however, were not discouraged in their many attempts to secure my participation; one of them even went so far as to sit in my lap. At last, they decided I was a no-goer and gave up.

In due course, Hicks and the other two descended the stairs and we left the parlor, Hicks marching and swinging his arms. He seemed in fine fettle; out on the sidewalk, he inhaled rich deep draughts of air, and pounded his chest. With fervor he declared: "That wretched disease is gone and I'm well rid of it!" He went on to describe in detail where he had left his disease.

We returned to the hotel and, next morning, to work. Hicks seemed to be in the best of health. I cannot endorse Hicks' system of therapy; I can only report what I witnessed, and there the matter must stand.

The Buckhorn Hotel served as the town's social center. The staff was efficient, if somewhat formal, and here I refer especially to the dining room waitresses. These were mature ladies of obvious respectability. They wore conservative dark blue dresses, crisp white aprons, and black low-heeled shoes. They performed their duties politely, but without cordiality. One evening, Robby Hicks tried to jolly up one of these ladies. She stared at him in puzzlement, raising her eyebrows; then she walked away, shaking her head, as if saying to herself, "Now I've seen everything." Later that evening, Hicks propounded a novel theory, which, all taken with all, seemed plausible. According to this theory, the ladies of Battle Mountain were segregated into rigid social classes. The social elite were employed as waitresses at the Buckhorn Hotel. Ladies of the lower classes worked elsewhere—some, even, at the Sunset Saloon.

In due course the Battle Mountain job terminated. Western-Knapp had no other projects starting up, and once again I

THIS IS ME, JACK VANCE!

became unemployed. My mother, meanwhile, had moved to an old farmhouse in the country near Oakley, along with my brother and sister. I was happy to join them.

For a time I enjoyed a period of idleness. I fell in love with one of my sister's friends, a charming dark-haired little imp named Jean. The affair, such as it was, went on for several months until her family moved off to Mendocino.

I had been reading P. G. Wodehouse, and so stimulated, I wrote a story, specifying a rather giddy summer resort as the locale. As I recall, the characters were silly; a lot of the story was improbable. In any case, I don't know whatever happened to this story. If I could find it, and if anyone wished to read it, they might do so, upon my receipt of $1 million.

During this period I listened to a lot music on the radio. The great swing orchestras were becoming popular. The magnificent Casa Loma Orchestra, which I revered then as I do now, was still on the ascendant, as was the Benny Goodman band.

My sister Patricia was a pretty girl, and she had boyfriends by the dozen. One of these was a trombone player named Orin Blattner, who, like myself, was captivated by jazz. Orin and I spent many pleasant evenings playing records and listening to the radio, although I suspect that his presence was half due to me and the music, and half to the opportunity it offered for mooning around my sister.

Tomato season started, and I found work at the Western California Cannery in Antioch, where truckloads of tomatoes arrived and were converted into catsup. There were several steps to this process: the tomatoes went first into a steamer, then after a certain amount of time fell out upon a conveyer belt which carried them to a discharge spout, where they fell into pans. These pans were distributed to ladies who removed the skins. The pulp was then compressed and the juice sent to a boiler, where sugar and vinegar were added, along with garlic and other spices, and in due course the result was catsup.

The job to which I was assigned required both vigilance and agility. I was required to catch the steamed tomatoes in a pan as they fell out of the spout. When the pan was loaded I would transfer it to the conveyer belt which took it to the ladies, first of course putting an empty pan under the spout. The tomatoes would emerge from the spout sometimes one or two at a time, other times in a great gush, and if I was not on the alert, they would overload the pan and pile up in a big mess on the floor. Every morning, at exactly 8 o'clock, the tomatoes would be put into the steamer. I lived nine miles from the cannery, and sometimes I overslept or was otherwise delayed, so I would ride my motorcycle at great speed into Antioch, skid into the parking lot, slam the motorcycle down, run through the cannery and throw a pan under the spout just in time to catch the first tomato as it rolled out. This happened to me more than once.

Tomato season ended; I worked a month at odd jobs. Then I had nothing to do until spring, when asparagus season started, and I went back to work at the cannery, where I lucked into a really pleasant job. I worked with four girls and a government inspector. Truckloads of asparagus would arrive from one of perhaps a dozen different branches; from each truckload a sample would be brought to the grading table, which the girls would examine for defective items. I then weighed the rejects and entered the results in a journal.

The asparagus season came to an end. My uncle informed me that Western-Knapp was starting up a new job near the town of French Gulch, just south of Mt. Shasta. I called the San Francisco office and was hired as a laborer, and told to report at once.

I had traded in my motorcycle, and now owned a Chrysler convertible, very sporty but rather long in the tooth. I drove north to French Gulch and took lodging at the French Gulch Hotel—which, by the way, is still in operation. At the Mountain King Mine, I became assistant to Sparky the welder, which meant carrying tanks of oxygen and acetylene up and down the steep hillsides—strenuous work.

The Mountain King Job lasted only for two months before I was laid off, but as luck would have it I learned of another job near the town Helena, which was about ten miles west.

This was a job unlike any I had ever held before. On the Trinity River, a doodlebug similar to the one I had seen on the mudflat near Kelseyville was in operation. It floated in a pond, and was held in position by four lines, two on either side, fore and aft. At the edge of the pond, a drag line worked, scraping material out of the bottom of the pond, lifting it and dropping it into the doodlebug hopper. The material would then be diverted into the chutes at either side of the boat, where it would be washed down over the riffles and ultimately discharged downstream into the river.

The work had been proceeding using two shifts, but now a third shift was added. The crew of each shift consisted of three men: the operator of the dragline, and aboard the doodlebug, the operator and the oiler. I became the oiler on the new third shift.

Duties were intermittent. I was required to keep the machinery of the doodlebug oiled and greased, then occasionally—usually not more than once or twice each shift—we would be required to move the doodlebug forward, which meant going ashore and shifting the lines to convenient trees, by which means we'd move the doodlebug into appropriate positions. I also used the bulldozer to move aside boulders and in general clear the area, so that the dragline could back up away from the pond when this became necessary. This again was a job which needed doing only once each or twice shift.

A week passed, then two weeks, and the work proceeded smoothly. One moonlit night, I went ashore to use the bulldozer to move rubble from behind the draglines. For no particular reason, perhaps an excess of zeal, I was carrying out this job rather farther than was necessary, perhaps a hundred or hundred and fifty feet behind the dragline. I turned around, and to my astonishment, discovered a vacancy where the dragline had been working. I took the bulldozer back, and found that the edge of the pond had given way. The dragline had fallen forward into the water, and was now totally submerged. The operator had jumped free and had reached solid ground, but of course was in a state of dismay, as was everyone else.

In the morning, the two partners who were the bosses and operators of the project, arrived and looked the situation over. They were not pleased. The problem was how to rescue the dragline from the pond and get it back on dry land. They conferred for a time, went away, and evidently used the telephone. About noon, two pickup trucks arrived with four men, whom I learned were lumberjacks, but also accomplished riggers. They unloaded equipment from the trucks: wire rope, several big blocks, pulleys, a pair of heavy slings, and now the rescue process began.

The first step was to engage the slings around the back axle of the dragline, which of course was submerged under six feet of cold, muddy water. The question then arose as to who was to dive down and put the slings around the axle; the owners looked around the group, and their gaze fell upon me. One of them pointed. He said, "Vance, you look healthy and ready for a swim, so grab up those slings and let's see some action."

Here I would like to make a digression in order to mention an episode from the work of Lewis Carroll, namely *Alice in Wonderland*. I refer to the occasion when Alice had eaten some of the mushroom and, having grown large, was crowded into the rabbit's cottage with her foot up the chimney. Outside, the folks were gathered around wondering what to make of the situation, and someone suggested that Bill the Lizard should be sent to investigate. Despite Bill's misgivings, he was induced to enter the house by the chimney. Alice, however, heard alarming noises and gave a sharp kick. The folks outside were now astonished to see Bill projected from the chimney and off through the air. I cite this case in order to mention that I now felt like Bill the Lizard while he was being urged to investigate the house.

Still, with the owner pointing at me, I would lose face if I failed to follow the instructions. Therefore, pretending non-chalance, I removed my outer garments, and taking one of the slings jumped into the water. It was very cold.

The slings were at last in place; I was out of the water, still quivering, but dry and dressed. The riggers now took over. They ran one end of the inch-thick wire rope to a stalwart tree and made it fast. The bight of this rope was passed through a block, and the other end was attached the other end to the bulldozer. The block was now engaged into the slings, so that when the bulldozer started up, its force would be magnified double.

So the process began—to no avail. The treads of the bull-dozer ground into the dirt. The riggers were not dismayed; they ran another wire rope to the same tree, brought it back, engaged the bight in another block, and attached this to the end of the first line. Now, the pull of the bulldozer would be magnified fourfold. The bulldozer set off, and the dragline was hauled inch by inch up from the pond. Once the dragline was secure, the owners fired not only the dragline operator, but also the opera-tor of the doodlebug, and me, though we were both blameless.

I collected my gear and drove into Redding, where I telephoned my uncle in San Francisco. He told me to wait by the telephone and that he would call me back. As it happened, that very morning, his friend Buck Finley had mentioned a small operation that was just starting up. An hour later my uncle called back and instructed me to drive to the Nevada City Hotel in Nevada City, and there report to Martin Lawley.

I obeyed these instructions. Mr. Lawley turned out to be a young engineer, intelligent, even civilized. He described the job. From a place named Sailor Flat, south of Nevada City, we would take a drill rig and lower it down some steep slopes to the bottom of a valley. There, we would set it up and start to prospect the soil in this area, which according to Lawley had never been prospected before. There were only three of us in the crew: Lawley, the drill operator, and myself. A pair of geologists, representatives of Buck Finley, would also be on hand. They would set up riffles to assess the amount of gold in what the drill rig extricated from this operation.

The next morning we drove south to Sailor Flat, where we found the drill rig mounted on the back of a truck, and the operator, Joe Poston. We scouted out the terrain, and immediately realized that it would be no mean feat to lower the drill rig to the bottom of the valley. In fact, it took us six days of digging, felling trees, making bridges, performing some artful rigging when necessary, gradually easing the drill rig down the slope and finally setting it up at the bottom. The next job was to bring water to the site so that the geologists could work their riffles. We built long flumes to water sources a hundred yards distant, and the prospecting began.

I could describe the drill rig in detail, but instead I will say only that it used three buckets—one about three feet in diameter, another about two in diameter, and another one foot in diameter, to accommodate different densities of soil. On each bucket were teeth, which dug into the soil. These were turned by a circular gear and weighted down by a heavy metal driving shaft.

The work went on for about a month and a half. We moved the drill rig here and there. I don't know what the geologists found in the riffles; they gave us no indication. I have the feeling that they were rather disappointed. Eventually they packed up their gear and left, and so the job closed down. This did not disturb me, since the tomato season was starting up and I had a job waiting for me at the cannery.

The catsup production, as I described earlier, took place in big stainless steel boilers using steam coils for heat. For every batch that boiled, a residue remained encasing the coils. It fell to me to remove this residue. This was not a pleasant job; the tools were steel wool, sandpaper, a chisel, a scraping edge, and oil. If I were not careful, I would scorch my fingers. In any event, I managed to perform this job satisfactorily.

The year was 1937, and I was twenty-one years old. The tomato season ended, and I enrolled as a freshman at the University of California at Berkeley when the fall semester started. Thus began a new phase of my life, unlike any which had passed before.

Clay lies still, but blood's a rover;
Breath's a ware that will not keep.
Up, lad: when the journey's over
There'll be time enough to sleep.
—A. E. HOUSMAN, *A SHROPSHIRE LAD*

CHAPTER 3

MY LIFE AT the university was for the most part pleasant and exciting but at times rather dreary, because I was chronically short of money, and often I had to resort to undignified expediences.

During my first semester, I worked in the home of Hamilton Wolf, an artist associated with the California School of Fine Arts, where I put in, theoretically, four hours a day of housework in return for room and board. The Wolfs were nice people, but the four hours per day became onerous, and for the second semester I lived in the basement of a sorority, hashing during meals, and doing odd jobs. The summer passed, and in the fall I had found enough money so that I could rent a room near the campus. I hashed for my meals at a fraternity.

I started the semester as a physics major. My classes included physics, mathematics, German, geology, and a required course of English. After a month or so, I changed my major for reasons which were perhaps frivolous. When I surveyed my classmates, I found them deadly dull and even a bit tiresome. I must mention that I started college not to secure an education, nor to train for a career, but for more or less social reasons. I did not fancy myself a typical college boy of the 1920s, in his raccoon coat, playing the ukulele, and ready to dance the Charleston at any provocation; but still, something of this concept lingered in my mind. In any event, I changed my major, first to English, then to journalism—not because I planned to become a reporter, but because I had joined the staff of the student newspaper, *The Daily Californian*, which presently became the focus of my existence.

The offices of the *Daily Cal* occupied the lower floor of Eshleman Hall, across the court from the Student Union. As a journalism major, I became eligible for a quasi-WPA job working for the journalism department. The job took little time and brought me in $60 a month. I won't describe the work involved in bringing out a daily college newspaper, except to say that it is not far less complicated than producing a real newspaper and that the student staff was (and probably still is) dedicated, skillful and efficient.

The staff organization was simple. The seniors were the editors, juniors the reporters, sophomores assistants to the juniors, and freshman consigned to dog-work.

On the *Daily Cal* staff at this time was a junior named Marjorie Higgins, who later became a famous war correspondent and who was launched somewhere over the Pacific. Also on the staff was a sophomore named Anita Whistler, who also became a war correspondent and who was shot down over Cambodia. Among the sophomores were two individuals with whom I would come to have a lasting association. The first was Anne Pickering, better known as "Pick," the daughter of an editor of a yachting magazine; the second was John West, a Berkeley native.

West's father was a realtor who had come into possession of a rather grand old Victorian house which, apparently, must be demolished to make way for new construction. So John, my brother David and I set to work taking this house apart, which we were supposed to do with great care in order to preserve the walnut paneling and black oak beams. John had thought of me as an effete impractical beer-drinking rascal, and was surprised to find that I was also a worker.

During this first semester I became part of a group—it was too loose and tenuous to be called a clique—that consisted of myself and three other habitués of the *Daily Cal* office: Don Matthews, Jim Tierney, and Jerry Edelstein. We all shared similar inclinations, which could most easily be grouped under the general term "revelry." These included beer-drinking, jazz music, and "staff parties" which occurred at an isolated site in the hills east of town. In addition to the beer, there was also singing of college songs, and general jocularity. Yet these by today's standards were quite innocent events, and great fun; no one ever had his feelings hurt.

Halfway through my second semester, an intense young fellow presented himself in the *Daily Cal* office. His name was Samuel Hayman Wainwright III. He was gaunt, dark-haired, narrow-faced, with keen aquiline features and blazing dark eyes, and he palpitated with nervous energy.

He came to the *Daily Cal* in search of publicity. He had organized the Thumbwaggers' Club, which was intended to expedite hitchhikers in their travels hither and yon. He laid out on the desk a T-shirt emblazoned with a black fist with the thumb raised in the hitchhiker's salute, and explained that he was organizing a stunt by which he hoped to excite public interest in the association, and to establish this T-shirt as the official uniform for hitchhikers. There would be two teams of two persons each; these would set out from Berkeley and hitchhike to Salt Lake City and back over the weekend.

The juniors came to interview Sam and wrote the story, so that Sam received his desired publicity. The story, when it appeared the next day, cited the names of those who were to participate in this challenging exploit. This was Wednesday. On Thursday, the day before event was scheduled to begin, Sam revealed that a member of his second team had backed out of the project. Sam was in distress. He looked here and there, and his eyes fixed on me. He said, "Jack, why don't you become a Thumbwagger, at least for this occasion?"

I thought to myself: Jack, once again the gods of chance have tapped you on the shoulder. So I agreed to Sam's proposal.

The next evening at 5 o'clock we gathered at the foot of University Avenue, the four of us all wearing Thumbwaggers T-shirts. Sam and his partner were up first, and within five minutes they caught themselves a ride. I and my partner, a pleasant fellow named Bob Wylder, went out to stand in the road; almost at once we too were picked up by a man who had read of the Thumbwaggers in the newspaper. Sam's strategy had borne fruit!

Sam and his partner, arriving at Reno, were picked up by an Indian towing a trailer. The Indian said that he was on his way to Salt Lake City, so Sam and his partner gladly jumped in the trailer. However, a few miles out of town, the Indian changed his mind, and turned south toward New Mexico, so that Sam and his partner were marooned at Sparks, Nevada. Bob Wylder and I reached Elko, Nevada, where we too were stranded, and could not catch a ride for love or money. We became discouraged, and Bob, making discretion the better part of valor, decided that we should return home.

Across the road was a Southern Pacific Railroad yard, where a freight train had just pulled in. We crossed the road, climbed the fence and approached a brakeman, from whom we learned that the train was heading west to Oakland. He seemed good-natured, so we moved down to the end of the train and climbed into the caboose, where we made ourselves comfortable. There was an iron stove to heat the car, but the fire was on the point of going out, so we opened the front panel and replenished it with kindling we found in a box. We sat down to rest and enjoy the ride. The train started to move.

Almost immediately a railroad bull entered the caboose. He saw us and bellowed, "What the hell are you two doing in here? Get out!"

We sidled past him to the back door, but the train was already moving at a good speed. We looked back with imploring expressions, but the bull showed us no mercy. "Go ahead," he roared, "jump!"

The train had picked up speed, and was now going at 15, maybe 20 miles an hour. But the bull pushed forward. "Jump!" he ordered again.

Wylder and I both jumped. We landed in a ditch, rolled over and over, scraping ourselves, but breaking no bones. Sitting up, we disconsolately watched the taillights of the disappearing train.

We sat for a few minutes, then picked ourselves up, climbed the fence, limped back into Elko, where we found a bus station, and, ingloriously, rode a bus back to Berkeley.[2]

When we arrived, we found that Sam and his partner had preceded us. We consulted together, and at Sam's instigation, decided to lie, so that in *The Daily Cal* there appeared a new story, to the effect that the two gallant teams of Thumbwaggers had both completed their epic journeys to and from Salt Lake City over the weekend. Sam, however, had lost his enthusiasm for the Thumbwaggers' Club, and we heard nothing more of the project.

During these years, when I found the time, I wrote science fiction. In my freshman year I wrote a long novelette, which I never submitted for publication, but which I later cannibalized.

2. I like many kinds of music besides jazz, including old folk music. An LP was recorded back in the '30s by Jimmy Rogers, "The Singing Brakeman." The tune which comes to mind was "Just Waiting for a Train."

I'm a thousand miles away from home
Just waiting for a train.

The emotion Rogers projects is very real. While I'm on the subject, I'd also like to mention another LP by Harry McClintock, better known as Haywire Mac. This was about cowboys and also the great American hobo. Nor must I forget Ukulele Ike (alias Cliff Edwards); one of his records is Stack O' Lee, one of the high achievements in jazz.

During my sophomore year, since I was still an English major, I took a course in creative writing. The professor was George Hand: a tall, saturnine gentleman, stern and doctrinaire. Each week we were required to submit some item of creative writing, which he would comment upon and sometimes criticize. A fellow student in the class was Don Fabun, who later became editor of *The Daily Cal.* He submitted a pastiche concerning a prize fight. I, on the other hand, turned in a short science fiction story which I thought I would submit somewhere for publication, but which in the meantime I thought would serve as my weekly exercise in creative writing.

The class convened. George Hand entered the room, marched up to the podium and looked around the class. He gathered his energy, and spoke with almost painful deliberation. "This has been a remarkable week," he said, "and I have been impressed by the breadth and scope of the submissions. I should note that they range up and down the gamut of excellence. On the one hand, we have a pungent account by Mr. Fabun, which takes us to the front seats of a prize fight. His sentences are terse and alive. We can smell the sweat; we can feel the thud of the blows; we know the thrill of victory and the pathos of defeat. It is a memorable piece of work. On the other hand,"—and here Professor Hand rapped the top of the podium with his knuckles—"we have an almost incomprehensible example of what I believe is known as 'science fiction.'"

The professor here allowed himself to show a small smile. "This sort of thing, perhaps unkindly, has been termed a semi-psychotic fugue from reality. I, of course, am not confident to make such a judgment."

After class, I threw away the story, which I did not like very much anyway.

The semester came to an end. I learned that Western-Knapp was starting a project at a tungsten mine near Bishop, in the eastern flank of the Sierra Nevadas.

I drove down to Bishop in a Model A coupé jointly owned by my brother and myself. The job was isolated in the mountains a good distance from Bishop, so the crew was lodged and fed on the premises at no charge. The superintendent was Eric Freitag. He took up residence in a small house adjacent to the work, where presently he was joined by his wife and—to my astonishment and delight—his daughter Dorothy.

At the first opportunity, I made myself known. This—to make a long story short—initiated a romance which lasted through the summer.

Here I must describe a pair of events of no particular consequence. The first of these was a rash act on my part. The other young bucks on the crew beside myself were Bob Magliano and Neil Holbrook. One day we were unloading sacks of cement from a truck, and for some reason entered into a ridiculous contest to see who could carry the most sacks to a platform. All of us carried two sacks without any problem, one on each shoulder, and Magliano carried three sacks, two on one shoulder, one on the other; I did the same, and I forget if Neil followed suit or not. Then, out of sheer bravado, I told the truck driver to put four sacks on my shoulders, two on each. He looked dubious, but shrugged and did so. I stood there with four sacks of cement on my shoulders, my spinal column feeling like a piece of overcooked macaroni, my knees knocking, and I staggered over and dropped the cement on the platform. Of course this was an idiotic stunt; I might have sprained something beyond repair. Luckily I didn't, although I am not too proud of this display of macho heroism.

The second incident occurred while I and one of the laborers were up on the hillside digging out a footing. It must be recalled that the year was 1939. While we were working, the news reached us that the Germans had invaded Poland and that war had started. For a moment we stood silent, awed by the thought of the carnage now in progress and the inevitability of more to come.

Summer passed, the job ended. Dorothy and her mother returned to Palo Alto; I never saw Dorothy again.

In the fall I returned to Berkeley. I was no longer part of the *Daily Cal* staff, since I had failed to make the sophomore cuts. Still, I spent most of my spare time in the *Daily Cal* office.

My usual cronies were John West, Don Matthews and Jimmy Tierney, otherwise known as Tiger. It was our habit to sashay down University Avenue to the Anchor Café, where we would indulge ourselves in the house speciality, Anchor Steam Beer. At more or less appropriate hours of the day, the cry might be heard, "Down to the Anchor for a tankard!"

At this time the appellation "red-assed" was in use. Red-assed meant dashing, daring, wild, ready-for-anything, let-it-all-hang-out. We considered ourselves a very red-assed group, and one evening at the Anchor, we conceived a very red-assed scheme. By some clever means, we would hoist a large red communist flag high up to the top of the Campanile.[3]

We acquired a bag of balloons, a tank of helium, a good deal of stout cord, and several other items, then set about to wait until the weather would seem to be propitious. The optimum weather conditions occurred almost at once when we arrived at a quiet, balmy evening with no prospect of wind. At midnight, after inflating a large number of balloons with helium, we crept out to the Campanile with our cord and supplies. At this time the campus was deserted and we felt inconspicuous. We encircled the Campanile with the cord, leaving it somewhat slack. To the plumb end of this cord we tied the flag.

The next step was to attach a hook, fashioned from a paper-clip, from which would hang a length of thread by which someone on the ground might control the balloons' rate of ascent and at the proper moment unhook the balloons by giving a jerk on

3. The Campanile, a 300-foot belltower erected in 1914, is to this day a symbol of UC Berkeley.

the cord. The flag, drawn in by the encircling cord, would hang as if from a flagpole.

This, as I say, was to be our next step. But at that moment, sad to say, our luck deserted us. Wind came first in a little puff, then a breeze, and finally as a gale. The balloons danced around crazily; some of them went into a holly tree where they burst, producing alarming noises. Not too far away was a night station where the campus cops rested, or played pinochle, or did whatever they did. Evidently they heard the noise, because they immediately emerged from the station. When we saw their flashlights and heard them running, we fled like frightened rabbits in all directions. Our wonderful red-assed scheme came to naught, although at this time it is pleasant to contemplate what might have been; one mourns the passing of youth.

Winter came and went, and when spring arrived I became bored with university life and decided that I was wasting my time. I heard that the navy was recruiting electricians to work at Pearl Harbor. I made inquiries and applied for a job as an electrician. To my surprise, I was hired and told to report to a ship at a certain date, which I did. I arrived wearing a suit and carrying a suitcase. I mounted the gangplank and asked the man on duty to direct me to my cabin. He laughed with sour jocularity. "Cabin? There's no cabin. Get your ass forward to the number one hold." I discovered that this was a troop ship and that we were being shipped over to Honolulu as if we were troops. Here was the start of my disenchantment with the navy.

The passage to Honolulu was by no means a luxury cruise. The cuisine was uninspired; we slept in bunks stacked one above the other; the bathroom facilities were grim and evinced no concern for ordinary sensibility. There was some gambling, and a few fights, but otherwise little recreation. In due course we landed in Honolulu. No one came aboard to cry "Aloha!" or throw leis around our necks.

We rode buses out to Pearl Harbor, where we were addressed by a functionary. He congratulated us upon the privileged status which we now enjoyed, although as I surveyed the group, I thought we seemed a rather shifty lot. He mentioned that accommodation was available in a nearby bunkhouse, with an adjacent restaurant, at moderate rates which he quoted. Since I would be earning 56¢ an hour, these rates seemed exorbitant. The functionary went on to mention that other places, more reasonable if less convenient, might be located in Honolulu proper. I immediately returned to Honolulu, where I consulted a newspaper and was guided to a pleasant room with kitchenette privileges a block behind Waikiki beach.

On the next morning, I rode the bus to Pearl Harbor and reported for work at the electricians' shop. The superintendent was a blond affable chap about forty years old named Ralph Honeychurch. He told me that much of their work was for the repair of gyroscopes, meters and other such delicate equipment. I told him that I could probably handle the work after I learned a few of the techniques. Honeychurch took me to the desk, gave me some tools, brought me a meter, and left me to my own devices. I took the meter apart, tested it here and there; I saw no broken wires or signs of dry rot. I located the adjustment screws and gave them a twist or two with my screwdriver and put the meter back together. I noticed no improvement.

For a week or two I sat at my workbench, achieving little or nothing. To pass the time, I polished candlenuts until they took on a beautiful gloss. Presently Honeychurch told me that they needed a man in the electroplating department, where he thought I might perform to better advantage.

I discovered electroplating to be interesting, although it was wet work, and there were acids and toxic chemicals to be avoided. Still, I did well there, and lasted two months.

Meanwhile, I was enjoying my life away from work. Every evening I went swimming at Waikiki Beach, and Sunday mornings I would breakfast at the Waikiki Tavern. This was an open-air restaurant between the Moana and the Royal Hawaiian. Here I had my first taste of papaya. I would sit over my coffee, enjoying the surroundings as if I were a wealthy tourist. Girls were a scarce commodity, due to the navy. I gave this matter a great deal of thought, and finally evolved a thesis, to this effect: If you want to find girls, you must go where the girls are.

I immediately put this theory to a test. In the newspaper I learned that the local theater group was casting for a play called *My Sister Eileen*. I showed up at the stipulated time and place and found that I was right; the place was swarming with girls. Just for fun, I tried out for a part but failed to make it. However, I cut one of the girls from the herd and arranged a social engagement. This took place on the following Sunday. I rented a car, picked up the girl, whose name I now have forgotten. We drove out into the hills to a nice restaurant, where we ate dinner, drank a bottle of wine, and the evening went along swimmingly. Yet this girl, while she was very pretty, was by no means the Queen of Sheba or Salome, and in fact was quite proper; so the evening ended on a formal note, and I never even kissed her goodnight. When I calculated the price tag, I was forced to conclude that girls were a luxury I could not afford, especially since I was trying to save money to pay for my passage home.

At the plating shop the work went slack, and I was transferred to the degaussing crew. "Degaussing" means canceling a ship's magnetic field so that it will not detonate nearby mines. To achieve this end, a gang of low-status workers is situated at intervals deep down in the hull next to the outer skin of the ship, where they sit like galley slaves, heaving on a cable to a regular beat, so that eventually they haul the cable completely around the hull of the ship. This is a miserable job.

I worked at degaussing for several weeks until I had accumulated enough money to pay for my trip home. I resigned from my employment at Pearl Harbor, and the navy gave me a "discharge with prejudice."

I boarded the Matsonia, and enjoyed the most idyllic cruise of my life. This was to be the last voyage of the Matsonia, and we arrived back in San Francisco about the first of December.

A week or so later, the Japanese hit Pearl Harbor. A somber thought sometimes occurs to me: if I had not departed as I did, I would probably still be there.

Along with the rest of the country, my life entered another new phase. In Richmond, Kaiser had opened a shipyard and was starting to build Liberty ships. I applied for work and pretended that I was a welder. They gave me a test to strike up a few sparks, and time after time I stuck the welding rods to the steel, so they ejected me with derision. I went to another building and, citing imaginary qualifications, was hired as a rigger. Riggers worked in conjunction with traveling cranes, which moved along tracks in front of the main fabrication shops. These were extremely heavy-duty cranes, capable of moving anything from single sheets to several tons of steel. Three such cranes moved along the tracks, each with four riggers and the operator, who sat in a cage high above the work. A checker designated which sheets of steel were to be moved. Two of the riggers attached appropriate harness to this steel—this would be either slings or clasps—and then signaled to the operator as to which bay the steel should be delivered. The other two riggers of the crew landed the steel, disengaged the harness, and the whole process began again.

As I mentioned, four riggers worked with each crane, one of whom was designated the leaderman. I was assigned to the number two crane, the one in the middle. The leaderman was Ted Lyon. We were an efficient crew and moved a great deal of steel, so that after three or four months, Lyon was promoted to be quarterman, which means ship superintendent, and I was promoted to be leaderman of the number one crane.

This was a job I enjoyed. I unloaded the steel with Jack Hart, a young man about my own age, while two older men whose names I forget worked in the bays unloading it. Hart was an engaging young rascal, and he and I became friends off the job. One of Hart's intimates was another young scamp by the name of Galen Fisk, who will long be remembered as the inventor of the Fisk System. This was a method by which Fisk prepared himself for a social occasion. He would fill the bathtub with warm water, remove his clothes, place on the rim of the bathtub a pint bottle of scotch, then immerse himself in the water. As he washed, soaped his hair, brushed his teeth, or did whatever else he did in the bathtub, he would take occasional nips from the bottle, so that after stepping from the bathtub, drying himself and dressing, he would find himself prepared for the evening.

About this time during my work at the shipyards, I learned of an army intelligence program based in Palo Alto, where qualified persons were to be instructed in the Japanese language. The program was not yet operational, but persons with previous acquaintance with Japanese would receive special consideration. Learning of this program I enrolled in evening classes at the University, where I became immersed in Japanese geography, Japanese history, Japanese culture, and of course the Japanese language, which I discovered to be complicated and difficult, not because of the grammar which is straightforward and even simple, but because the Japanese speak in idioms, which must be memorized. The written language, which can be characterized as calligraphy, is unique, perhaps at times illogical to the western mind, but at all times fascinating.

For a moment I will digress and attempt to explain the intricacies of the Japanese system of writing. There are two syllabaries, each of which includes about thirty symbols. Each symbol corresponds to a monosyllable, such as *ka*, *ma*, *ne*, *mo*, *fu*, and so forth. One of these syllabaries is known as *katakana* and is used to transcribe foreign words and names, special technical terms; it is also taught to children as their first means of writing. The other syllabary is *hiragana*, which is used in ordinary Japanese writing, usually in connection with the root characters, called *kanji*. There are many thousands of *kanji*; I am not sure of the exact number. They were originally derived from the Chinese, but adapted to the Japanese language, and each defines a concept. Each *kanji* character must be accompanied by a tail of perhaps two or three *hiragana* symbols to denote its grammatical function.

The Japanese are a complex folk. One of their cultural traits is an almost mystical appreciation of, and devotion to, beauty—everywhere, and in all forms. This includes the writing of the *kanji*, which is often accomplished by the use of brushes and ink.[4]

There were eight of us in the class, but I remember only two of them with any clarity: Max Knight, who worked at the University of California Press, and Mary Chapman, the eighteen-year-old daughter of missionaries. Mary had spent six years of her life on Hokkaido, the northernmost island of Japan, and already knew a smattering of Japanese. She was tall, slender, healthy and just short of pretty. Yet she carried herself with a style all her own, the elements of which were wholesome innocence, cheerfulness, artlessness, and an innate conviction that everyone she encountered was as virtuous and decent as herself.

4. The older the ink, the greater its value. The best ink is often several centuries old. It would have been formulated by an ink-maker, lain aside, the stock inherited by the ink-maker's son, who would keep it and pass it down to his own son in turn. This stock of ink would be passed down from son to son over the generations, until finally it might be used. Such ink would be sold as a black cake in a porcelain pot, and reverently stroked with a damp brush.

To write a character properly, an exact sequence of strokes must be observed. If the strokes are not carried out in the proper order, the educated eye can see that the character is malformed, to the shame of the person who has performed this gauche travesty.

As a side illumination, and to draw attention to my own achievements (on the theory that if I don't no one else will), I would like to mention that I became quite deft in the writing of the characters and was so complimented by my instructors.

Everyone liked her, including me, although our relationship never exceeded simple friendliness—to my regret, although I made one or two perfunctory attempts. Even now I sometimes take time to wonder how her life went.

At the Kaiser shipyards I continued to work with Ted Lyon on the number two crane. Every day, after we had sent off steel to the bays, there would be a wait of several minutes. I took advantage of this time to practice my Japanese calligraphy, chalking the characters on steel plates. The steel then went into the fabrication shops, where the workers no doubt wondered as to the significance of these cryptic markings. I half-expected that someday I would look up to find a pair of hard-looking gentlemen in black suits bearing down upon me with the intent of capturing the ringleader in a spy system. However, nothing of the sort ever occurred, and I continued to practice Japanese calligraphy without interference.

At this time Lu Watters' Yerba Buena Orchestra was starting to attract attention. On Monday nights, the band rehearsed at an isolated roadhouse high up in the hills above Oakland known as The Big Bear.[5] I attended these sessions as often as I could manage, often in company with my friend Don Matthews, and with my current lady-friend. As I think back, I can only marvel at what intensely romantic evenings these were. When the Yerba Buena jazz band became popular, playing five nights a week at the famous and fabulous Dawn Club, I was there as often as not, standing in front of the bandstand, letting the music blow my hair back. The band subsequently moved to Hambone Kelly's in El Cerrito, a town to the north of Berkeley. The personnel included Lu Watters and Bob Scobey on trumpets, Turk Murphy on trombone, Bob Helm on clarinet, Wally Rose on piano, Clancy Hayes or sometimes Harry Mordecai on banjo, Dick Lammi on tuba and Bill

---

5. Lu Watters later composed a tune, "Big Bear Stomp," in recollection of these sessions.

Dart on drums, all of whom rank in the highest echelon of jazz musicians.

In the spring of 1942 my friends Don Matthews, Jim Tierney and Jerry Edelstein all graduated from the university. Don married Sally Lee, and later they worked for Kaiser in the front office. Sally's friend Betty married a fellow named Glen Slaughter. During the summer Glen and Betty approached me and asked if I was in the market for a car. I was, so they sold me a Cadillac sedan for $400. Later they jeered at me, and made as if they had cut a fat hog in the ass. The Cadillac, however, functioned flawlessly and I had no complaints.

My friend Jack Hart lived in an apartment on Ellsworth Street in Berkeley. We arranged that he should drive me to work one week, and the next week I would drive him to work. It seemed a logical procedure, but half the time while I waited for a ride, Jack Hart would never show up, and I had to jump in the Cadillac, drive to Ellsworth Street, wake him up, and drive like mad to Richmond so we could get to work on time.

One day I noticed a cornet hanging in the window of a pawn shop. I went in and bought it, and so embarked upon my lifelong effort to become a competent jazz musician, an effort in which I have had varying degrees of success.

This first cornet was pitched in the key of B, not in the usual B-flat. The postman heard me practicing, and offered to trade me his B-flat cornet for this rare B cornet. I accepted, and the B-flat is the cornet which I own to this day.

In 1943 the draft went into effect. Like everyone else, I had registered for the draft, but had been told that my work in a critical occupation placed me in a deferred classification (although for a fact, due to my rotten eyesight, I was probably 4-F anyway). A few weeks later, however, I learned that the situation had changed and that I was no longer deferred. Soon, I feared, the draft board would be calling. I thought things over for a week or two, then went to San Francisco and joined the sailors' union. After a short period of training I received papers which certified me as an ordinary seaman. Two days later, I boarded my first ship and began my maritime career.

Ship me somewhere east of Suez,
Where the best is like the worst,
Where there ain't no Ten Commandments,
An' a man can raise a thirst.
—RUDYARD KIPLING

CHAPTER 4

I SPENT THE duration of the war aboard ships, first as an ordinary seaman, then as an able seaman. To say that I entered upon a new phase of my life is to utter an understatement so flagrant that the words would seem to tremble on the page. However, I will state simply that life at sea was unlike anything I had ever known or even suspected.

As a rule, seamen enjoy a great deal of spare time. I used this spare time to write, and much of what I wrote was subsequently published in one form or another.[6] I sold a set of fantasy stories to Hillman Publications, who issued the collection using the title *The Dying Earth*. I also wrote a mystery story, which was published as *The Flesh Mask*, and a frothy bit of foolishness to which the publisher attached a wildly misleading and inappropriate title, *Isle of Peril*. My original title was *Bird Island*, which was suggested to me by a cartoon appearing in one or another magazine. The cartoon depicted a yacht full of tourists passing

---

6. I did much of my writing in a deck chair where I could look off across the ocean. On a calm day in the tropics, the view across the ocean trivializes any attempt to describe it in words. There are endless miles of blue water, transparent at the swells, gently heaving all the way out to the horizon, where maybe a few cumulus clouds are mounting.

a little island swarming with seagulls, pelicans, and many other species of birds. The guide, addressing the tourists, remarks: "On the right, you will notice Bird Island."

The story generally concerns itself with the misfortunes of Rexie, a cat belonging to Mr. Coves, owner of a hotel on the island. One day Rexie is chasing a mouse; the mouse disappears around a corner. Rexie, pursuing the mouse, rounds the corner to find himself facing not the mouse but a baboon, the pet of a guest at the hotel. Rexie, though puzzled, believes that the mouse by some mysterious trickery has taken on the semblance of a baboon. With this conviction in mind, he pounces upon the baboon, hoping to dispel this peculiar illusion. But the phantasm persists, and Rexie is dealt a sound thrashing.

Yet Rexie persists in his belief that the baboon is the mouse in disguise, and every time he encounters the baboon he attacks this phantom creature. On each occasion he is thoroughly trounced.

By reason of these episodes, Rexie becomes disturbed and disconsolate. For solace, he sneaks down to the cellar, where Gaston the chef is ripening a vat of curds for cheese. One day Gaston, descending to the cellar, discovers Rexie indulging in a repast of the maturing cheese. The indignant chef seizes Rexie and hurls him into the middle of the vat. Rexie is forced to swim to the edge of the vat and flees upstairs, sodden with sour-smelling curds.

The routines aboard every ship are the same. There are always three watches, from 4:00 to 8:00, 8:00 to 12:00, and 12:00 to 4:00. There are three men to a watch: one ordinary seaman and two able seamen. Additionally, there are a bosun (or boatswain, or bo'sun), a day-man (who works eight-hour shifts), and a carpenter. The three men take turns steering the ship, which is a rather tiresome task. The quartermaster, as the acting helmsman is known, stands in front of a compass, watches as the needle moves to one side or another, and makes appropriate adjustments with the wheel. Back in the chartroom is a device called a tattletale, which charts the ship's deviations from its projected course. The good quartermaster's chart will show a relatively straight line with only a few minute zigzags; mine was always the worst of the crew, and resembled an oscillogram.

The crew is divided into three groups: the deck gang, the engine room gang, and the stewards. This is not to mention the officers, who are a group apart. The crew dines in one mess hall, the officers in another, with the galley between. Everyone eats out of the same pot, as the saying goes, and the cuisine is always good. I've never been on a ship where the food was bad.

To ship out aboard a new ship is always an adventure, since you never can foresee the nature of the men with whom you will be spending several months of intimate association. Seamen, so I was quick to discover, are highly individualistic, if not often peculiar. It is something of a marvel that they are able to adapt to each other. This is accomplished through the use of a set of unspoken rules of conduct. When the ordinary seaman first comes aboard the ship, he is unaware of these rules, but he quickly learns them.

First coming aboard, a new arrival makes a cautious survey of the crew, trying to winnow the affable and good-natured from the surly and truculent. Some of the crewmen will seem easygoing, happy-go-lucky, good-fellows-all; others may appear to be reserved or even aloof. Yet I found that at the end of a voyage these aloof ones were often the persons whom I grew to like and respect the most, while those who seemed so agreeable turned out to be rascals.

My first ship was a C3 cargo ship. On this trip the cargo happened to be troops bound for Australia. When I first came aboard, I was informed that I must undergo a medical examination to determine my state of health. I suspected that I could not pass the eye examination, so I memorized the eye chart, which

I remember to this day: E; F B; L P E D…As a result I had no problem outwitting the medics.

I drew the 4 to 8 shift, which I found to be the most desirable of the three. Deck work doesn't start until 8 o'clock, and stops at 5 o'clock, so anyone on the 4 to 8 shift is required to put in only one hour of deck work, which is often unpleasant, dirty, and even miserable.

Arriving in Australia, our first landfall was the port of Townsville, where we discharged the troops, and where I went ashore on foreign ground for the first time. I visited a pub, where I was served Australian fish and chips and Australian beer. The authorities are extremely strict in regard to closing hours. At 5 o'clock in the afternoon the bars stop serving beer. About quarter to 5 every night occurs what is called the swill session, when everyone present lines up behind the bar and starts drinking beer as fast as possible. The bartenders at this time dispense with the beer pump; instead, they walk up and down behind the bar with hoses and spray beer into the tankards. Heaven knows who owes money and who doesn't. In any event, I enjoyed the spectacle.

The ship returned directly to San Francisco. My next ship was a C2 cargo ship, and its destination was once again Australia. At Gladstone, a port somewhat south of Townsville, I was wandering aimlessly around the back streets and came upon a group of men standing under a lamppost. They were playing a game they called "Two-Up." Its rules are as follows: The first player—I will call him "A"—has two coins. The second player, whom I will call "B," bets upon whether the coins, when tossed into the air, will come down both heads or both tails, or whether they will come down mixed. "A" then throws the coins high up in the air—ten, fifteen feet, twinkling in the lamplight, then coming down to hit the dirt. Everyone crouches to see whether "B" wins or loses. Offhand, it would seem as if this game were entirely one of chance, but these fellows practiced long hours learning how to throw these coins in such a way so as to influence how they alighted, thereby frustrating the bet. Their success with this feat seemed uncanny.

I joined the group and bet a shilling on pairs. The coins went flickering up into the lamplight, came down, struck the dirt. They were not pairs; I lost my shilling.

The next day was Sunday. A chap on my watch named Walt and I went ashore to find that the pubs were closed. We then met with an adventure which even today causes me to cringe at my own foolishness.

Walt and I encountered a young man and asked if he knew where we could buy a bottle of scotch whiskey. He told us that he himself could provide such a bottle—at a cost of £10. We each gave him £5. This fellow told us to wait where we were and disappeared into a nearby house. Walt and I waited; and we waited; and we waited. Finally we knocked on the door of the house. A little girl about nine years old opened the door. We asked what had happened to the fellow who had entered a while ago. The girl laughed. "Oh, him. He ran through and went out the back way. You won't see him again."

So I learned never to place my trust in the blandishments of an unknown purveyor. I now realize that this was a cheap price to pay for such a salutary precept.

While at sea, a member of the watch is required to proceed to the bow and there stand lookout. If he sees anything unusual, he must immediately notify the mate on the bridge. During the day, the first intimation of any approaching vessel is when the tip of the cargo masts show above the far horizon. Some seamen have an astonishing eyesight and are able to see these mast-tips, which are no larger than specks. This capability far exceeded my own flawed eyesight. Even when an approaching vessel seemed about ready to collide with us I might fail to take note of it. When this occurred, soon there would follow a telephone call from the mate on the bridge.

"Vance, why didn't you report that ship?"

To this I had a standard response: "The ship was in plain sight; I felt sure that you'd already seen it."

"Of course I had seen it. From now on, report everything in sight—even if it's nothing more than a sick seagull!"

"Yes, sir."

Lookout at night was a lonesome and tiresome hour and twenty minutes. A passing ship would be noticed only if its running lights were visible, and at any distance these tended to merge into the atmosphere. In any case, ships in the middle of the Pacific were rare, so that excessive vigilance seemed to be something in the nature of overkill.

My third ship, which was a Liberty, was probably built by Kaiser in the yard where I had worked as a rigger. I had brought my cornet aboard with me. Whenever I stood lookout at night, I thought to put this otherwise wasted time to some useful purpose. I would bring my cornet to the bow and practice scales, arpeggios, play a tune or two, and generally strive to improve my technique.

One calm night the captain happened to be out on the bridge while I was running up and down the scales. The captain cocked his head to listen, turned to the mate and said, "What in the world is that noise?" The mate pretended to listen, and said, "It seems that Vance is practicing his cornet." So ended my attempt to enhance my musicianship on company time.

The *Katarina* crew included two individuals of notable quality and strange dispositions—or perhaps there were three, if laughingly, and with modesty, I include myself. The first was the captain, Karl Reisendorf, and the second was Gerald Britt, the bosun.

Capt. Reisendorf reminded me in certain respects of Eric Freitag, the Western-Knapp superintendent, perhaps because both demonstrated traces of a Teutonic background. Captain Reisendorf was about fifty years old, burly and stalwart but not at all fat; his dark hair was cut *en brosse* in a style like that of a Prussian *Junker*. He carried himself with what I shall describe as austere deliberation. He was uncommunicative, and when he spoke, he used terse, gruff sentences in response to which any question or doubt was unthinkable, much as if Moses were to ask God to please repeat the Third Commandment, since Moses wanted to be sure that he had everything straight, and could God perhaps speak a bit more slowly and carefully, if he did not mind.

On first knowing Capt. Reisendorf he would seem portentous and grim. As the voyage proceeded, however, the full scope of his character became evident. It turned out that he had a practical and even rather casual philosophy, to wit: If the thing works, don't fix it. His theories were distinctly his own, and if the world did not like them, the world knew what it could do. When finally we left the ship in Charleston, South Carolina, I had come to admire and even revere this doughty captain.

Initially, the *Katarina* sailed through the Golden Gate and out into the Pacific. The typical speed of a Liberty ship was about eight or nine knots, and voyages tended to be of considerable duration. In due course we arrived at Ulithi Atoll. We entered the lagoon through the pass and dropped anchor and awaited further orders. Around this time I developed a severe toothache, apparently in one of my wisdom teeth. A navy boat picked me up and took me to a navy hospital ship. There a navy dentist pulled out the ailing tooth, and for good measure he took out my other wisdom teeth as well. This dentist was extremely efficient, and I have the navy to thank for this particular item of dental surgery, all at no cost.

One day the captain ordered a fire drill. The lifeboats were unchocked, lowered into the water, and rowed about for a bit, then hauled back aboard the ship—all except for that boat manned by the bosun and about six of the crew. This particular boat was powered by a gasoline engine, and the bosun seemed to enjoy driving it about the lagoon, because after a while, instead of returning to the ship, he set off to the west and disappeared from sight. This was outrageous conduct, which could only have been conceived by Gerald Britt, the flamboyant bosun. Capt. Reisendorf glared after the retreating lifeboat, then shrugged and retired to his quarters.

Two hours passed, then the lifeboat returned to the ship. The bosun no longer looked jaunty—in fact he had a rather hangdog droop to his head. The crew, whom he had dragooned, were furtive and looked over their shoulders up toward the bridge to see if the captain was watching, but he did not appear. The boat was hauled aboard and dropped into its chocks. The chief mate then summoned the miscreants to his quarters, where they were all docked a day's pay. However, they were not logged, which is to say that their names and exploits were not recorded in the log book. The punishment, in short, was light. It appeared that Capt. Reisendorf had considered the situation, and deciding that no great harm had been done, he had elected to avoid a sensational display of authority.

The *Katarina* finally left Ulithi and sailed first to Townsville, then after discharging cargo continued northeast to Malaita, one of the Solomon Islands, and there dropped anchor a quarter-mile offshore.

The chief mate, probably in order to keep the crew occupied, called in the bosun and instructed him to slush the rigging. This, of all the deck work, is probably the most disagreeable. The bosun compounds a heavy semifluid substance consisting of fish oil, creosote, tar, and anything else he can think of. The cargo masts are secured by staves consisting of inch-and-a-half wire rope running from transverse spars near the tops of the mast, port and starboard, to the deck. Slushing is intended to protect the rigging from the corrosive effects of salt water, and it may well do so, for all I know. The process is not complicated: the bosun's chair is shackled to the stay, and is controlled by a line running down to the deck. The chair is hoisted aloft; the man with the slush bucket climbs aboard and proceeds with the slushing, which means that he dips a rag into the brew and wipes it upon the rigging. Meanwhile, down on the deck, his partner lowers him at an appropriate rate. On this occasion, I was aloft in the bosun's chair. My line was tended by a man named Fini, who was not a profound thinker. When the bosun yelled, "Knock off for lunch!" Fini dropped the line and made for the deck house, while I came sliding at speed down the rigging. I landed in a tumble with the slush bucket in my lap. Fini, sheepish and apologetic, ran back and helped me to my feet.

After the slushing, the crew was put to work painting the side of the ship just above the waterline. To this end, a raft was lowered into the water and a line, known as the frapping line, secured it to the side of the ship. While engaged at this work, it was necessary that the painters be constantly wary of the sewage outlets, which opened from the hull about ten feet above their heads. Signs were always posted in the head, saying: "PLEASE DO NOT FLUSH THE TOILET—WE ARE WORKING BELOW." But like as not these signs were ignored, and as we worked there might occur a sudden deluge from above.

The water here was clear and green. We saw no evidence of sharks, and so spent a great deal of time swimming off the side of the ship. Sometimes, diving deep, I could look clear under the hull of the ship, and I was tempted at times to swim under to the other side, but was always deterred by some primal fear.

We finally received sailing orders, and hoisting anchor sailed north to New Guinea, where we unloaded about half of our remaining cargo. Then we swung south to Brisbane, where we unloaded the other half. Leaving Brisbane, we set off to the east across the Pacific, but our destination was not San Francisco but South America. We learned that we would be at sea for twenty-seven days; it would be the longest passage of any I had known.

After about a week at sea, during the 8 to 12 watch, I did something to annoy the bosun. I've forgotten what it was—

something trifling, as far as I was concerned. However, the bosun, who was generally unstable, flew into a sudden rage, and instead of knocking off the crew at five minutes to 12, kept them working until exactly 12 o'clock. Aboard the *Katarina* I was union delegate for the S.U.P., and I remonstrated with Britt.

Strange events occur at sea, and I had heard rumors of macabre incidents and tales of folk who had gotten on someone else's nerves, and who had disappeared leaving no trace. In all candor, I was afraid. Was I destined to end my life at this early age? I felt especially vulnerable standing lookout in the bow, and spent more time watching over my shoulder than searching the sea for approaching vessels. But nothing ever happened, and I heard no alarming sounds. Meanwhile, the bosun ignored me, but I was not reassured and remained on the alert.

One day, Britt and I worked aloft on the transverse spar of the No. 2 cargo mast. Britt, busy at something, looked over his shoulder and instructed me to go to the far end of the spar, drop a line and haul up some tools. The deck was forty feet below. I thought, "This is it—no way!" I pretended to be busy and caught hold of the mast. Britt, muttering in annoyance and disgust, went himself to the far end of the mast and dropped the line. I breathed a sigh of relief: had I wished, I could have tapped his shoulder and sent him plunging forty feet to the deck. No man wishing to kill another man would have placed himself in so vulnerable a position.[7]

The *Katarina* was a slow ship, and idled at a stately eight knots across the ocean. Each day was like every other, and time lost its meaning; but eventually, the imminence of landfall hung in the air, and everyone aboard began to stare forward across the bow hoping to detect the first loom of the continent.

Yet the days passed and the sea remained empty, until one morning a shadowy layer of what appeared to be mist lay across

---

7. In fact, at the end of the trip Britt told me that when taking stock of the crew he considered me the least shifty of the lot!

the eastern horizon. As the hours passed, the mist took on color and substance, and finally contour. At last this was revealed to be a great mountain range: the Andes.

As the *Katarina* approached the coast, black jagged crags rose up to awesome heights. The base of the mountains was splotched with what appeared to be bird droppings. The details gradually became distinct, and the splotch became a town— namely Tocopilla, where the *Katarina* would take on a cargo of nitrate. At Tocopilla there was a single loading dock, now occupied by another vessel, so that the *Katarina* dropped anchor a hundred yards offshore to await its turn at the dock. Almost at once a flotilla of rowboats put out from the shore. As they drew near, the hucksters aboard jumped to their feet, gesticulating, shouting slogans, and waving bottles in the air. Aboard ship, any seaman who wished to obtain one of these bottles tied a dollar bill to a line and lowered the line into a boat, where the huckster exchanged the dollar bill for a bottle, which was then hoisted back aboard the ship. Here the cork was removed and the contents tested, where they usually proved to be brandy of tolerable quality. And so began the Saturnalia.

Tocopilla was not a large town, nor particularly impressive, being dwarfed by the Andes rearing behind and by the expanse of the Pacific in front. There was no agriculture and the local economy subsisted upon the sale of nitrate from guano, as well as the entertainment of visiting seamen. To this latter end, a number of hospitable young ladies were ready to solace any forlorn or homesick sailor whom they might encounter wandering at loose ends along the street. Few of these ladies spoke English, but this was no handicap, since all were adept at sign language and mathematics. It should also be noted that alcoholic beverages were everywhere available, including wine, beer, brandy, gin, vodka, the legendary Pisco rum, and what was locally known as "Scotch whisky." This may or may not have been distilled in Scotland, but it was probably not a product of Chile.

Public order in Tocopilla was maintained by a corps of stern and uncompromising policemen who patrolled the streets. They wore brown semi-military uniforms and were clearly not to be trifled with. If they came upon a seaman committing a nuisance, they would not hesitate to hustle him off to jail, where he might pay a $5 or $10 fine—or, if he was howling drunk, he might be sequestered overnight and released in the morning. Some of the town ordinances were bewildering: for instance, a man and a woman were not allowed to walk side by side; one must precede the other. If a couple wished to promenade in civilized fashion, they might well be apprehended and fined. I myself never ran afoul of this particular law; however, as I rambled about the town inspecting local landmarks, ingratiating myself with the population, I took aboard considerably more Pisco rum than was necessary, and in the process generated the king of all hangovers, from which I did not recover for three days.

Meanwhile, the *Katarina* had shifted to the loading dock, where it was now taking on cargo. I finally became restless; time was passing, and I felt obliged to go ashore once more, although on this occasion I would indulge in no more wine, beer, or even Pisco rum. Nor would there be any further raffish antics of the sort which had enlivened our first hours in port.

I went ashore in company with a young seaman named Tom Cogsdale, who was civilized, of easy disposition, and a year or two younger than myself. His current mood was much like my own: languid, depleted, and not disposed to further revelry.

At the southern end of town was what passed for an upper-class district. There were two churches, a grade school and an almost imposing high school, a market, a pharmacy, and a sprinkling of fine residences—and also an old-fashioned soda fountain. Tom and I, wandering along the main street, discovered the soda fountain, and entering, seated ourselves at one of the two tables, which seemed more comfortable than the stools along the counter. An old man in a white smock served us ice cream sodas, and we sat brooding over the events which so far had befallen us during our time ashore. After a time the door opened, two girls entered the shop and seated themselves at the other table. They were perhaps eighteen years old; they wore white blouses, dark skirts, white sandals: evidently the costume of high school girls. Both were clearly the daughters of upper-class families, and both were decidedly pretty, each in her own fashion. The brown-haired girl was pert, vivacious and conceivably more extroverted than the slender, black-haired girl, who showed a thoughtful, almost wistful expression, as if she were caught up in a charming daydream. She might be said to have resembled an illustration in a pre-Raphaelite book of fairy tales.

These events occurred many years ago, and I cannot pretend to exactitude in every detail or every trifle of conversation, which in any case would be irrelevant. Suffice it to say that in the next few minutes Tom and I roused ourselves from our malaise and set about making the acquaintance of these two girls. I will also point out that both Tom and I wore clean, neat, socially acceptable garments, that neither of us could be considered notably ill-favored and raffish vulgarians, and that we both conducted ourselves with an old-fashioned gallantry, to which only a vestal virgin might take exception.

Both girls knew a few words of English, and Tom and I remembered something of our high school Spanish, the use of which caused the girls amusement. Nevertheless we managed to communicate adequately.

The brown-haired girl was Miranda, we learned, and the black-haired girl was Laura. Both had double-barreled or hyphenated last names, which indicated that their families had pretensions to aristocracy. Both girls were graduates of the local high school, and hoped to start the coming semester at the university of Chile in Santiago far to the south. The parents were not in accord with this program. Here it should be noted that among upper-class South American families arranged marriages were still common practice. To such unions both Miranda and Laura were in opposition, since they seemed an unfair infringement upon their destinies.

The sun was dipping into the Pacific, and dusk had started to fall over the town. Both girls were friendly but neither flirtatious nor forward. Still, we asked them if we might take them to dinner at some nice restaurant of local reputation. At this proposition the girls became ruefully amused; their parents, so they stated, would be outraged to learn of the escapade, for fear that the girls' reputations had been irretrievably soiled.

A sudden idea occurred to the girls, and they conversed back and forth in rapid Spanish, which neither Tom nor I could understand. Then Laura told us that there were no fine restaurants in town, but that they knew of an interesting spot down the coast which they would be happy to visit. If we hurried, we might dine at this restaurant and be back before their parents returned from the social event at which they were engaged this evening. We went out into the street, where I flagged down a taxi; we all climbed aboard, and Miranda gave instructions to the driver. He looked over his shoulder, shrugged, and said, *"Muy bien, señorita—¡vamos!"*

The above account is not significant in itself, and is only a precursor to subsequent events. I must inform the reader that most of the evening's impact derived from the landscape, and that there are no sensational or erotic climactics to this episode. Nevertheless these events still haunt me whenever I think of Tocopilla.

The road south was a poorly maintained track of compacted sand and gravel flanking the shore, curving in and out to avoid the Andean crags which thrust high into the sky. The moon was at its full, ripe and round; it illuminated what was at once a mountainscape, a landscape, a seascape, a jagged and irrational chiaroscuro. A fringe of white surf came and went along the pale beach; in the water beyond rose sawtoothed ridges of black rock, twisted spires, isolated reefs, at intervals creating coves and small bays.

After fifteen miles or so we arrived at the restaurant. The kitchen, outdoors, consisted of a grill over a bed of hot coals and a nearby worktable, both under a canopy. Five or six tables fringing the beach were available to patrons. Tom and I and the girls seated ourselves at one table, and the taxi driver went to another at the far end of the beach, where he evidently expected to dine alone. On this evening no one else was on hand, and a middle-aged lady served us fish, potatoes, a bottle of white wine, all of which were extremely good. The girls were anxious to return home, so we wasted no time staring out to sea, but rather paid the bill, which was not at all exorbitant.

We climbed aboard the cab and returned to Tocopilla, where the girls were pleased to arrive home early enough to avoid the censure of their parents. We took leave of them with polite shakes of the hand and no more, a situation which caused me a fit of depression since, I must admit, that in the course of the evening I had become enamored with Laura. As I watched her disappear behind the door of her home, I wondered whether we should ever meet again, although I realized that this was not likely. We were ships that passed in the night.

On the afternoon of the next day, the *Katarina* put out to sea and Tocopilla dwindled astern.

Here I include a final note in regard to our stay. As I mentioned, the local police were both vigilant and rigorous. Certain members of the crew were apprehended and put in jail once; several of them were put in jail twice; but only one member of the ship's crew was jailed three times. This was none other than Captain Reisendorf! As he was being released from his second stay, he crossed the street and, feeling an urgency, urinated against a tree. The police immediately dragged him back to jail.

We sailed north to the Panama Canal, passed through, crossed the Caribbean to Charleston, South Carolina, where we discharged our cargo of nitrate. The crew was paid off and started home.

I rode back to California by bus, and waited about two months before shipping out again.

My next three ships were all tankers. On each occasion I signed on as quartermaster, which meant no more, or very little, deckwork. I always hoped to find a ship fitted out with an iron mike—which means that a gyroscope steers the ship and that the quartermaster has little to do but chat with the mate on duty—but I was never this lucky, and so had to stand at that wheel four hours at a time.

Once, while putting into New Orleans, we approached along a narrow canal. I was at the wheel; the pilot was looking forward calling instructions. I veered a bit to the right; the pilot called out, "Easy left." I complied. The pilot looked ahead, and said more sharply, "Easy left!" I complied again; the pilot looked ahead again. The pilot at last looked over his shoulder and cried out: "*Haaaaard* left!" In my concentration, I had been giving him easy *right* on each occasion, with the banks of the canal only a few feet to either side.

Perceiving my previous mistakes, I did as commanded, and the ship did not run aground, for which both the pilot and I were thankful.

Aboard another tanker, the *Verendrye*, I obtained some luminous tape and, for no particular reason, created a star chart on the overhead of our forecastle, with the major constellations, the first and second magnitude stars picked out accurately. The captain, learning of this enterprise, came down to the forecastle, lay down on his back, looked up and marveled at this unprecedented creation. At the end of the voyage, he gave me a glossy photograph of the ship signed with his name and best regards. I still have this photograph and am naturally very proud of it.

My third tanker ship was the *Mission Dolores*. To allay the tedium of the voyage, I built a still, using copper tubing, assorted pots and pans, and a garbage bucket to hold what was called the "swipes," consisting of dried apricots, water and yeast allowed to ferment. Surprisingly, I produced what turned out to be some rather good apricot brandy. On the homeward voyage, the captain chanced to explore the forepeak, where he discovered the still and became enraged. He confiscated the works and tried to identify the perpetrator, without success. I stood at the wheel while the captain raged back and forth with the mate, vowing all manner of penalties upon the depraved bootleggers, which would be meted out as soon as the ship reached port. Meanwhile, I stood at the wheel quivering at every threat.

When the *Mission Dolores* pulled into Long Beach, a coast guard ship came alongside and one of the midshipmen shouted, "Have you caught that villain who made that still yet?" I sweated new trickles of blood.

We docked, and soon enough the coast guard officers came aboard. They took the still, examined it carefully, and to preserve any potential fingerprints sealed it into the bonded locker. During the evening the captain had some friends aboard for a party. After a few drinks, the captain decided to show his friends what scoundrels he had aboard. He broke into the bonded locker and displayed the still. In the morning the coast guard returned aboard, and were astounded to find that someone had broken into the bonded locker. This was a grave offense. As for the still, it could no longer serve as evidence, since it had been much handled. So instead of catching the culprit, they excoriated the captain for the more serious offense of breaking into the bonded locker.

An hour later we were paid off and went ashore. I felt as if I had died and gone to heaven, and I resolved never again to become a criminal: a pledge which I have naturally honored in every respect.

I shipped out again twice, then decided that I had had enough of the sea and came ashore.

Darkling: A Threnody
by L. Bassington Mulliner
Black branches,
Like a corpse's withered hands,
Waving against the blacker sky:
Chill winds,
Bitter like the tang of half-remembered sins;
Bats wheeling mournfully through the air,
And on the ground
Worms,
Toads,
Frogs,
And nameless creeping things;
And all around
Desolation,
Doom,
Dyspepsia,
And Despair.
I am a bat that wheels through the air of Fate;
I am a worm that wriggles in a swamp of Disillusionment;
I am a despairing toad;
I have got dyspepsia.
—P. G. Wodehouse

CHAPTER 5

My mother now worked at Montgomery Ward in the foreign mail-order department. She was diligent, conscientious, and had built up what could be called a clientele, especially with missionaries in the Far East. Her salary was adequate, and with what I sent her she was now living quite comfortably.

With nowhere else to go, I moved in with her, at least temporarily. I was still solvent with funds from my last payoff, and now devoted myself to writing, trying to making a living wage doing so, but without notable success. I realized that my funds would soon run low and that I would need to find some sort of day employment which would allow me to write at night.

One day I ran into Sam Wainwright who, it may be remembered, was the organizer of the Thumbwagger exploits. Sam was as frisky and bright-eyed as ever, and he told me that he had become a carpenter's apprentice, work which paid reasonably well and which would in due course allow him to become a journeyman carpenter. The only disadvantage was that he had to go to school for four years in order to learn the trade. Still, he said, it wasn't so bad, and if I liked, he would take me to the union hall and introduce me to the qualifying officer.

The union officer, who apparently took his job casually, asked me three questions.

"What's the size of a sawhorse?"

I said well, it was about like this, like that.

He said, "Okay…Why are studs placed at sixteen-inch centers?"

This I knew. "That's so that the sheet of four-foot plywood will fit the studs correctly."

"Correct."

The third question I forget, but it might have been something like "Which end of a nail goes in first, the sharp end or the flat end?" I replied that I thought it was most likely the sharp end.

"All right. Sign here."

He gave me some papers, and I learned that now, by dint of my command of the subject, I had been signed on as a journeyman carpenter, bypassing the whole apprentice program.

I made no complaint, and went out in the corridor where Sam asked me how I'd made out, and whether I had passed the apprentice test. I said, "Yes indeed. In fact, I've qualified as a journeyman." Sam's congratulations were sparse.

On my first job as a carpenter I lasted two hours before I was fired. On my second I lasted until noon. On my third I lasted all day, and thereafter I managed to hold on to the jobs. In time I became a competent rough carpenter. It was only later, after teaming up with various German and Scandinavian craftsmen, that I learned the elements of finish carpentry. This is interesting and often delicate work, at times requiring the skills of a surgeon, but rewarding for anyone who can cut the mustard.

On one job, my presence on the premises was required only to satisfy some legal restriction, and I had nothing to do except wander here and there about the property. One day I approached the back fence and looked over, and saw a very pretty girl sitting on the porch of a house petting a cat. She seemed happy and gentle and playful, and I could not help but wonder if she might be induced to play with me. To make a long story short, I found that her name was Norma, and that she was happy to know me, and in due course we were married.

At first we stayed with my mother on Ellsworth Street. My mother had been going to night school, where of all things she had been learning the essentials of pottery. One night, just for fun, Norma and I joined her at her class. We got our hands into the clay, and after that there was no looking back. We joined the class, and produced a few odds and ends—dishes, ashtrays, one thing or another—and we were so pleased with the results that we set off upon what I now perceive to be a totally idiotic project, namely "Ceramic Center." This was a shop on College Avenue where we sold clay, glazes, plaster-of-Paris, and slip, which is liquefied clay. I built a kiln and we did firings for our customers. One of our friends, Dave Miller, contrived a beautiful sign for us, but the shop became more of a social hub than a profit-making enterprise. One night I was playing a jazz record and in walked Bob Mielke, the great jazz trombonist, and this is where I first met him.

We found a pair of partners, Jim and Mary Walsh, who conducted classes. But still our expenses far exceeded our income, and so finally we turned the shop over to the Walshes and set off on our first trip to Europe. Such was our acquaintance with the art of ceramics, and in retrospect I see how foolish we, a couple of tyros, had been to think we were qualified to run such a business.

Norma was strongly supportive of my writing from the start, and we began to work together as a team. I cannot emphasize enough how hard Norma worked over the course of my career—certainly as hard as I have, if not more. In these early days, however, the writing wasn't enough to support us, and I continued to work day jobs.

On one such job at Berkeley High School, I encountered a laborer named Red Sears who, using a cynical and sardonic appraisal, took me for a live one. We got to talking boats. He told me of the *Snoop*, a fine traditional wooden-hulled cutter. He stated that the owner would listen to any reasonable offer. Red would take me to inspect the *Snoop* anytime I so wished.

I accepted, and after work Red took me down Dwight Way to a vacant lot, where I saw the *Snoop*. It was a hulk about twenty-eight feet long and obviously in the last stages of decrepitude. I turned upon Red in disgust and asked him where was the boat which he had described. He had the grace to look off into the sky.

Nevertheless, Red introduced me to the boat's owner, Tom Hand, who with his wife Joanna lived in a house nearby. They were a rather bohemian pair, and I took to them; in time I brought Norma to meet them, and we became a congenial group.

Six months later the Hands decided to move north to Mendocino. Norma and I had been living with my mother, but in rather cramped conditions, so we were happy to rent the house which the Hands had just vacated.

I can't remember what became of the *Snoop*. I suppose it must have been hauled away at some point. We used the vacant area for a vegetable garden.

Norma and I acquired two cats, Pete and Joe. We also acquired a magnificent Packard sedan in perfect condition.

At the house on Dwight Way we hosted many parties and sometimes jam sessions. At one these sessions we met Al Hall, an excellent guitar player, who subsequently joined us in many exploits. We are still in contact with Al, even though he too now lives in Mendocino. One of Al Hall's business ventures was the creation and sale of compost. For this purpose he used redwood sawdust and fish guts, which he obtained from a cannery. In his front yard there were two impressive mounds of the ripening compost, which attracted swarms of flies beyond belief. Al also kept chickens, which dined on the maggots, and once he served Norma and me scrambled eggs for breakfast. I found that I could not eat these eggs, knowing that they were the product of chickens nurtured on maggots. When the compost was ripe, Al packed it in sacks, which were labeled "Al's Best," with Al's likeness in profile below.

Norma's parents lived in Colton in southern California, and whenever opportunity offered we would drive down and spend time with them. On one occasion I had an experiment in mind. I was selling stories on a more or less regular basis, but the returns were not astronomical, and I thought to improve the situation by becoming a "million-word-a-year man." I knocked out two stories in two days, the first of the Magnus Ridolph set. I sent the first drafts, without revision, to my agent Scott Meredith in New York. He sold them at once with no apparent difficulty. So much for the experiment. I was moderately pleased with this sudden gush of productivity, but I realized that in the long haul my temperament was not suited to this method of writing. I returned to my old system, which meant first draft, second draft; and if I were lucky I would find this second draft acceptable.

Just then, I received startling news from my agent. 20th Century Fox had picked up one of these stories, "Hard Luck Diggings," for compensation which at the time seemed phenomenal. Furthermore they invited me to write a treatment and possibly a screenplay at an inordinate weekly salary, if I would report to Hollywood at once.

Norma and I jumped in the Packard and drove south. We presented ourselves to 20th Century Fox, where we were introduced to Julian Blaustein, the producer. I was installed in an office with my name on the door in gold, a secretary, and told to get to work.

We rented a spacious house with a swimming pool in Coldwater Canyon. Every morning I drove to my office at Fox and tried to produce the kind of material which Blaustein expected of me. In truth I found this sort of work unfamiliar and not particularly agreeable. For one thing, the money, while gratifying at first, frightened me a little: I did not want to become dependent upon sucking at this golden tit.

Luckily, my fears came to naught. Julian Blaustein was promoted to become an executive producer, and all his projects were shelved. I was told, "Don't call us, we'll call you." The golden letters of my name were scraped from the door, my secretary bade me farewell, and everything else was restored to as before I had arrived. Without overmuch regret I took my leave of Fox Studios.

With the money we had accumulated during this stint in Hollywood, Norma and I embarked on our first trip abroad. We left our Packard parked under a pepper tree at my father-in-law's house in Colton, covered with a tarpaulin to protect it against the weather, bird droppings and other such depredations, and consigned it to the care of Norma's father. He undertook to guard it against recreational use by Norma's brothers, who were notably irresponsible. Norma's father guaranteed to exercise full vigilance in this regard, and we were reassured.

We made our way to the east coast, and at New York boarded a ship of Dutch registry. After a pleasant voyage across the Atlantic we disembarked at Southampton, England. Here we bought two bicycles, convinced that the most romantic and charming way of visiting the English countryside was aboard a bicycle seat. I can now state that under certain circumstances this is undoubtedly true; under others…not so true. However, I must remark that all during the time we were pedalling along the English lanes, we encountered nothing but sunshine, nary a drop of rain, which considering the dire reputation of the English climate seemed almost an act of divine providence.

As we traveled, we became aware of two curious facts. The first concerned food. A common vegetable served with lunch at cafés was cauliflower, usually boiled or perhaps steamed. Almost more often than not, we discovered among the stalks a plump white worm of such color and appearance so as to be hardly distinguishable from the vegetable itself. These garnishes were inconspicuous unless one examined the dish quite carefully. We often speculated as to how many inattentive customers had consumed one or more of these worms.

The other fact that came to our attention had to do with innkeeping practices. We usually spent our nights at bed-and-breakfast establishments, where we discovered that certain landladies changed their bedsheets only after every third or fourth guest. It became our habit that when we were first shown to a room, we immediately examined the bed; if we found that the sheets were not fresh, we quit the premises on the instant, without regard for the outcries of the landlady.

This was the late 1940s, and prices in England were comfortably low. The lowest for a night's lodging might be 7s/6d,[8]

8. 7 shillings, 6 pence.

but more commonly the going rate would be 10s, and occasionally 10s/6d, which still amounted to approximately $2 or $3. Breakfasts were usually sufficient to send the bicyclist along his way well fortified, consisting of corn flakes, bacon and eggs, bread fried in the bacon fat, and fried tomatoes.

We traveled to Winchester in Hampshire, then west through the New Forest before turning north into Wiltshire. Arriving at the town of Marlboro, we discovered that all accommodations were occupied owing to a convention, and we were obliged to ride twenty miles further along, up hill and down dale, to the town of Pewsey, where we were gratified to find comfortable lodgings.

The next day we rode out across Salisbury Plain. Toward the end of the afternoon we noticed some odd structures protruding over a nearby ridge, and gaining the top we looked down upon Stonehenge. Of all the routes by which one can approach Stonehenge, I consider this the most dramatic of all. There was nobody at hand, and we explored the premises alone. That evening we lodged at a country inn nearby, and in the morning set off to the north, ultimately to arrive at Oxford.

We spent a day or so exploring the quadrangles of this old city. But here at last we concluded that cruising England on two wheels had lost its romance, so from Oxford we set off south toward London.

We stopped for the night at an inn. After dinner we repaired to the bar where we met a pleasant gentleman drinking a mug of what he declared to be his favorite tipple. This, so he explained, consisted of Guinness stout mixed with port. He urged us to test this libation for ourselves, if only to enhance our own life experience. I was drinking Bass Ale and declined; Norma did not wish to hurt the gentleman's feelings and gave an indecisive response. The gentleman, thus encouraged, signaled the bartender, who put a glass of dark syrupy liquid with a fringe of foam at the top in front of Norma. She sighed, squared her shoulders, and with true American pluck lifted the glass and gulped down several swallows of this liquid. Here, motivated by gallantry, I draw a screen of secrecy over the ensuing events, some of which took place on the street and over the gutter.

On the next day we continued south and in the evening rolled into London. We checked into a Bloomsbury Hotel near the British Museum, then spent several days exploring London aboard the wonderful double-decker buses: Covent Garden, Hay Market, Picadilly Circus, Bond Street, Portobello Road, Mayfair, Soho…names of magic. One evening we dined at Simpson's-in-the-Strand, an extraordinary restaurant dating from the early 19th century. When a customer enters he is seated at a table, then is approached by a server wheeling a hooded cart, in which reposes a magnificent joint of roast beef keeping warm over a bed of coals. The server slices off slabs of roast beef which he serves along with dishes of potatoes and leeks; then, in a quiet voice he says, "And if you fancy a bit more, you need only signal and I shall be pleased to assist you—but!—*you must not waste.*"

Needless to say the roast beef was beyond reproach, and Simpson's was indeed a splendid restaurant.

The next day we took lunch at the Savoy Grill, situated in the Savoy Hotel, which has been long considered one of London's finest hotels, along with Claridge's, Brown's, The Dorchester, the Connaught and The Ritz. This is the same Savoy Grill where Bertie Wooster entertained his various fiancées and where "aunt bellowed to aunt like dinosaurs across a primeval swamp." The exploits of Bertie Wooster are chronicled in the books which have Jeeves in the title, such as *Very Good, Jeeves*; *Right Ho, Jeeves*; *Carry On, Jeeves*…all masterly works which validate my opinion that Wodehouse was one of the finest writers of the 20th century. This is perhaps not a fashionable opinion, but as the reader may have already deduced, few of my opinions are fashionable.

Wodehouse wrote little poetry, but his verse, such as it is, in my opinion transcends many an effort to extoll the virtues of a grecian urn. As a reference, here I will quote two lines from the first stanza of "Good Gnus":

When cares attack and life seems black,
How sweet it is to pot a yak.

And in the last stanza occurs this couplet:

And one more gnu, so fair and frail,
Has handed in its dinner-pail.

I hope that any of my readers who are not conversant with Wodehouse will instantly bury themselves in these marvelous works.

Neither Norma nor I wished to explore the continent of Europe on two wheels, so we sold our bicycles, boarded a train, and departed England. We bypassed France and rode directly into Austria and debarked at Innsbruck. At this point we were ready to settle down for a time and produce some profitable words. This would establish the program we would subsequently follow in many future excursions. We would find some romantic spot, rent a house or apartment, and there work sometimes as long as two or three months turning out a novel or set of stories.

At Innsbruck, taking local advice, we boarded a strange little trolley which reminded us of the Toonerville Trolley, and rode fifteen miles south into the Alps to a picturesque mountain village, Fulpmes. There was nothing much here except the Hotel Lutz, a shop or two, and a few houses built in the traditional Tyrolean style of bare evergreen boards, so that the village smelled of fresh pine and fir. We adopted *en pension* accommodations at the Lutz and were accorded a room on the second floor with a balcony. I remember this balcony well; it became my habit to sit in the sunlight on it while I wrote. One day a bee stung me.

We remained at Fulpmes a month or so while I completed several novelettes and started *Vandals of the Void*, a boys' book commissioned by Winston Publishing. At last we thought that the time had come to move on, so we returned via the funny old trolley to Innsbruck, boarded a bus and rode to Salzburg, where we spent a night or two in an inn once patronized by Mozart, then continued on into Vienna.

In Vienna we heard no music, however we rode the ferris wheel in the Prater amusement park, dined in the Rathauskeller, this being a restaurant in the basement of the Rathaus, or city hall. We visited Schönbrunn, the Habsburg Palace, notable for a great deal of *chinoiserie*.

We spent three weeks in Vienna. One day, when I was dressed in what little finery I had brought with me—namely gray flannel slacks and a dark blue coat—Norma took my picture. This picture is not in our photograph album. It shows me smiling placidly into the camera, while the photograph reveals that my fly was unzipped. *Sic transit gloria mundi*. This phrase is perhaps not totally appropriate, but it will serve. In any case, we presently departed Vienna by train, heading south toward Venice.

At Klagenfurt we failed to change trains as we were supposed to do, in order to avoid being swept south to Trieste and beyond into the wilds of Croatia. At the last minute we discovered our mistake, and with suitcases in both hands we leapt from the moving train and managed to catch the proper train into Venice, which we found beautiful beyond even the rhapsodies of the tourist brochures.

Leaving Venice, we rode south through Florence, Rome and into Naples where we met Gwen and Tony Griffiths and Gordon Tongue, whom, so it later turned out, we would know for years to come through many adventures and vicissitudes. They were typical of the English vagabonds who, on small fixed incomes, roamed the continent seeking out romantic places where the sun was warm, the atmosphere cosmopolitan, and the wine inexpensive.[9]

Norma and I revealed to our new friends that we were on our way south to Sicily. They told us that they had been living in Positano, which they described as a picturesque fishing village eleven miles down the coast from Sorrento. They spoke of it in such terms that we were induced to visit Positano ourselves.

Boarding a bus, we were conveyed south around the Bay of Naples, past Vesuvius and the isle of Capri, past Sorrento, and eleven miles south along the Amalfi road to a wide amphitheater sloping down to the beach with pink, green, blue, and white houses festooning the sides. On the beach was a hotel, Bocca di Bacco, at which we subsequently lunched from time to time, whenever we could afford to do so.

Norma and I were instantly charmed, found ourselves an apartment, and went to work, continuing with *Vandals of the Void*. I must again emphasize that in this work Norma was indispensable, and that she worked as hard as I did in producing this literature, if I may call it such.[10]

About the time we had completed *Vandals of the Void*, Gordon, Gwen and Tony left Positano for the Channel Islands, and Norma and I decided to join them there.

Arriving in St. Helier on the isle of Jersey, we took lodging at the Sandranne Bed & Breakfast. Gordon worked at a pub near the Gorey Castle. We took a photograph of Gordon jumping off a six-foot wall, and the camera caught him in mid-air, his legs splayed, his arms outspread, his coattails flapping, his face set in a grimace of anticipation of the shock to come.

---

9. Much of the popular music of the time, especially that produced in England, reflects this mood. Here I refer to those splendid orchestras of Lew Stone, Ray Noble, Ambrose, and the vocals of Al Bowlly. At this time Noble and Bowlly recorded such tunes as *Café Continental, Isle of Capri, South America Joe, One Night in Monte Carlo, Good Night Sweetheart, The Very Thought of You,* and many more.

10. Years later, I used Positano as the locale for a murder mystery, *Strange People, Queer Notions.*

This is a fine photograph that makes me laugh every time I think of it.

At the center of St. Helier is the Star Hotel. This is a rambling old Tudor structure, housing a venerable pub. One afternoon I chanced inside, where I found Gordon. He introduced me to a Mr. Lightbody, a gentleman of obvious distinction, whose varsity accent and tweed jacket identified him as a member of the British upper classes. He was blond, fair, blue-eyed, and almost handsome; his expression was bland and droll, and he might well have served as the model for Dorothy Sayers' Lord Peter Wimsey. Later I learned from Gordon that Mr. Lightbody was a fellow of Oxford, where, to use a British idiom, he had read literature, the classics and sociology.

At the moment of my arrival, however, Gordon and Mr. Lightbody had been engaged in a somewhat less scholarly exchange: namely, that of naughty limericks.

I tried to join their exposition of this noble art form, but my sparse repertory was soon exhausted, and I could only sit fascinated as Mr. Lightbody described the young man from Derwent, then next told of the daring musician named Bratt, to be followed by Gordon's reminiscences regarding the young lady in France.

Gordon and Mr. Lightbody ultimately paused for breath. In the general conversation that followed, Gordon mentioned to Mr. Lightbody that I was a writer, which prompted Mr. Lightbody to describe his doctoral thesis. This he described as an analysis of British society with specific emphasis on propriety, manners, decorum and all the aspects of conduct which controlled every phase of British existence. I expressed interest in the topic, and Mr. Lightbody expanded somewhat on the nature of this work. Here I will try to reproduce the thrust of his remarks as best as my memory serves me to do.

"The ordinary Englishman," said Mr. Lightbody, "is controlled by convention almost from the instant of his birth.

This control becomes more rigorous as the years proceed. As a child he learns to use his table instruments not as bayonets or tomahawks, but with delicacy and finesse. He is taught to leave a bit of food on his plate 'for Mr. Manners.' And so it goes. But despite all, certain solecisms remain. He notices how his parents will use their forks upside-down and pile food on them in a great mound, only to convey this loaded fork to their faces. Yet it is to be hoped that a properly reared person will learn to avoid this particular habit, and in due course acquire mastery of all the intricacies of etiquette, so that finally when he reaches his majority he has become a standard Englishman."

In a rather wry voice, Mr. Lightbody went on to say that he might, at some future date, expand his thesis into a full-fledged book on the subject, not merely as a catalogue of these conventions, but as a practical guide to help the individual use the quirks and unpredictabilities of proper conduct to his advantage.

I never saw Mr. Lightbody's thesis, nor do I know if his book ever materialized; but while writing this memoir, and thinking back on the Oxonian gentleman with the taste for dirty limericks, I was overtaken by a sudden impulse to compose my own modest example of what might have been. The result (I don't know what to call it—essay? vignette? article of fiction?) conjectures what perhaps we would have found in Mr. Lightbody's seminal work, supposing he had shared it with us that afternoon at the Star Hotel pub. I include it, perhaps improperly, in this, my autobiography, although it is completely imaginary and does not relate to any real events in my life. Still, I cannot resist.

🌿

Mr. Lightbody rifled through the manuscript for several moments, his slender aristocratic fingers ultimately alighting upon a page perhaps halfway through.

"Ah, yes," he said. "This section concerns the conventions of dress—which, I may say, are extremely rigid. For instance, it is considered extremely gauche for a dedicated pacifist to wear a regimental necktie; and the cad who sports white socks with black shoes may not be horsewhipped on the steps of his club, but still he will be considered a damned outsider. Again, only a Martian fresh from a flying saucer would don anything but a topper at Ascot."

Mr. Lightbody pushed the pages across the table. "Look these over, if you're of a mind to do so."

He busied himself with his tankard of ale while I glanced over his notes. I came upon some sheets entitled:

The Pervasive Influence of Protocol,
Propriety and Politesse in the British Isles,
and How Best to Use Them to Enhance Social Status
(A Practical Guide)
by Arthur M. Lightbody

I read through the text at first casually, then with increasing attention, and finally with the wonder of a chemist who has suddenly come upon a molecule of water with the formula HO_2. Here, of course, I exaggerate, but the reader must decide as to how much and to what degree.

Naturally, I cannot reproduce Mr. Lightbody's words with full exactitude, but I suspect that the gist of his advice will be clear enough. If among my readers are persons of extraordinary innocence or sensitivity, I suggest that they read only *Divisions I* and *II*, but avoid *Division III*. However, should they choose to read the entire section, I suspect that they will incur no lasting psychological damage.

Division I. In this section, Mr. Lightbody discussed first the black tie supper, then the more formal white tie dinner party, and the subtle distinctions between the two rituals, and also the quaint if somewhat old-fashioned tradition of the ladies rising from the table at some signal from the hostess while the gentlemen remain to smoke cigars and drink port and perhaps indulge in risqué anecdotes.

Division II. Here Mr. Lightbody discussed cutlery, napery, crystal and other items of table service, and how they are to be used. Great importance was attached to the proper handling of the ordinary dinner fork versus that of a fish fork, salad fork or cake fork; the correct and appropriate use of other utensils was likewise stressed. "The poor fellow who uses his butter knife to bisect his *Filet de Sole à la Vassant,*" Lightbody cautioned, "will discover that he has been roundly snubbed as a consequence."

Division III: Social dilemmas, solecisms and their most appropriate mitigations. "Now," wrote Lightbody, "we must address a problem which at some time or another has been a source of distress for us all. I refer to the gradual accumulation of gas in the abdomen which induces an ever-increasing discomfort. Eventually, and despite alterations of posture and ever more intense muscular effort, a powerful impulse occurs destroying all restraint, so that a flatulence ensues, often with a trombone-like sonority.

"This, then, is the situation. How best to deal with it? First, the person under discussion—let us call him 'Mr. A'—must by some means attempt to mitigate the solecism. An attempt at facetiousness, such as a gay and giddy laugh and a cry of 'Whoops—hahaaah!' cannot be recommended, since it will only cause Mr. A further embarrassment. A more subtle system of dealing with the predicament must be employed.

"Luckily, there is such a system, but it requires rigorous self-discipline.

"Mr. A must sit absolutely motionless for five seconds, with a mild, slightly rueful expression upon his face. Then, with eyebrows raised a trifle, he glances sidelong at the person seated immediately to his right, but for one or two seconds only. Then he returns to as he was before. This bit of byplay, needless to say, will not go unnoticed—and, if nothing else, will at least cause puzzlement and doubt among the other dinner guests. The person seated at Mr. A's right hand will also notice these circumstances, but now, taken off-guard, can only sit in a state of inanition, the expression on his or her face a frozen mask concealing fury, embarrassment and a sense of helpless futility. Other guests, motivated by sympathy and decorum, will now resume their interrupted conversations and presently all will flow as before. Mr. A will find that his solecism has now been ignored and that all is well—except that he will find that any cordiality which may have existed between himself and the person at his right no longer exists."

I had hoped to profit from a few more of Mr. Lightbody's elucidations, but the gentleman looked at his watch and exclaimed that he was late for an appointment. Rising to his feet, he gathered up his manuscript, dropped it into his briefcase and departed, coattails flapping, leaving Gordon and me to sit drinking beer and discussing Mr. Lightbody's remarkable work.

❦

There is no question but that Mr. Lightbody was an extraordinary person. The next day he left Jersey, and Gordon and I never learned what had become of him.

It was time for Norma and me to resume our homeward journey. We took leave of the Sandranne Bed & Breakfast, Gordon, Mr. Lightbody and the Star Hotel in Jersey, and traveled to Paris, where we would spend two or three days before taking the boat train to Le Havre. We thought to look up Stefan, the painter we had met in Positano, and learned that he was ill in the hospital. We rushed to visit him, and found him recuperating from a kidney stone operation. He insisted that we go to his studio and inspect his work, which was being assembled in preparation for a show. He gave us the address and telephone number of his patroness, who agreed to meet us at the studio and show us the paintings. We followed these instructions, took ourselves to this address, rang the bell, and the door was opened by a middle-aged lady, nicely dressed, gray-haired, who welcomed us into the studio and showed us the paintings. Then she served us tea. This was Stefan's patroness. Her name was the Baroness de Rothschild!

It now amuses me to mention that while we were in Paris for a few days, we only met one person there.

"Oh?" comes the question, "Who was that?"

"Didn't I say? It was the Baroness de Rothschild."

So then—never mind the raised eyebrows, nor the sidelong looks of incredulity; these are the bare cold facts.

We had arrived in Paris practically broke, with only enough money to keep us alive and take us to the boat train. Stefan's girl-friend, Claire, insisted on showing us the Parisian night life, a plan to which we were forced to accede. She took us to a cabaret where we were obliged to buy brandies, thereby using the money we had reserved for our meals. Thus thanks to Claire's hospitality we nearly starved during the rest of our stay in Paris. On the transatlantic voyage back to the States, we had no choice but to slink off the ship without tipping the stewards and waiters, who doubtless must have pegged me for a cheap SOB.

We checked into the Royalton Hotel opposite the Algonquin, where we scraped together enough money to buy ourselves beer at the bar. We dined on the free peanuts. Next morning we went to the office of Scott Meredith, my agent, where we were happy to learn that there was money waiting for us, as well as an offer of new work. Euphoria! I was sent to the office of Olga Druce, television producer.

You must wake and call me early, call me early, mother dear;
To-morrow 'ill be the happiest time of all the glad New-year;
Of all the glad New-year, mother, the maddest merriest day,
For I'm to be Queen o' the May, mother, I'm to be Queen o' the May.
—TENNYSON

CHAPTER 6

OLGA DRUCE WOULD play a large part in our lives for the next year or two. She was about forty, of middle size, dark hair, not bad-looking, with a perpetually cagey expression. She was obviously a woman who knew what she wanted. Currently she was the producer of a television serial known as *Captain Video and the Video Rangers*. She was not happy with her current crop of writers and was looking for an infusion of style and dash, so Scott Meredith sent over some science fiction writers, myself included.

When I arrived at her office in New York, I found myself part of a group which included Robert Sheckley, Arthur C. Clarke and a few others. Robert S. Richardson, a notable astronomer from Palomar Observatory in southern California, would later participate in the program, but was not yet on hand.

Arthur Clarke, so it developed, was uninterested in television scripts, and in the end, only Bob Sheckley and I joined the *Captain Video* team. The pay for an episode was $1,500, which at that time was quite a bit of money.

Norma and I rented an apartment and I set myself to writing *Captain Video* scripts. My first one was a great success; Olga Druce was delighted. I don't know how Sheckley made out. Incidentally, Sheckley is a first-class writer; he used to live up in Seattle, but I haven't seen much of him over the years.

It was summer, and the heat was fearful. Finally, after two months of suffering, I arranged with Olga that we should return to California and continue writing scripts from there. After shopping around, I bought a Willys Jeepster, a sporty little jeep convertible, and Norma and I drove back to California through Canada. We visited the Banff Hotel at Lake Louise, then drove south through Idaho, Nevada, and into southern California, through San Bernardino and Colton, and up Grand Terrace to the home of Norma's family. Here we expected to find our magnificent Packard awaiting us. We drove up the hill and into the driveway, and there, sure enough, under the pepper tree, was the Packard. Or was it the Packard? There was something there, no question about it, and it rather resembled the automobile we had left behind, in the care of Norma's father, but at the same time it looked like nothing we had ever seen before. The body was all dents, windows were broken, the tires were flat. Closer scrutiny did reveal that it was a depredated version of a once-beautiful Packard. Clearly, Norma's father had allowed her brothers to vandalize our beautiful car until finally it gave up the ghost. Norma, of course, was frozen in outrage, and she let everyone know about it. I was utterly shocked, but I restrained my emotions and said nothing whatever. Oddly enough, none of the miscreants mentioned the situation, much less apologized. The atmosphere remained chilly and we left Colton on the following day.

Norma and I visited my mother in Berkeley, then explored the countryside, and finally settled into an old farmhouse in the hills near the town Kenwood. I set myself to producing *Captain Video* scripts.

For a time all went well. I turned out scripts, and our only difficulty was that our telephone connection to New York was terrible. Olga Druce's voice sounded like a little squeak, so when I wanted to talk to her I had to go into town.

A reporter from the *Santa Rosa Press Democrat* interviewed me, and the story, when it appeared in the paper, carried the following headline: *SCIENCE FICTION WRITER IS FLYING SAUCER EXPERT!* This of course was ridiculous, since we had not discussed flying saucers at all. The reporter's name was Frank Herbert.

The summer passed. We had many visitors: my mother, my brother and my five nephews, along with some musicians— Dick Oxtot, Bob Mielke, Ellis Horne, and also Tom Hand, Earl Sears and Red Sears. It was often party-time at the old farmhouse. I bought a Rolleicord camera and took some beautiful pictures. I also became fascinated with the lore of kites and their construction. One of these was a kite about six or seven feet across and shaped like a child's paper airplane. When it was finished I took it out into the field and arranged to fly it. It flew beautifully, went straight up in the air, way up high in the sky, then, like the dart it was, turned and darted toward the ground and killed itself.

Meanwhile I was having ever more trouble with Olga Druce because of our inadequate telephone service. Finally she ordered me to come to New York, which I did. There she gave me a special commission: Richardson, the astronomer, had submitted a script which she found unsuitable. There is a natural phenomenon known as the *zodiacal light*, which is a hazy blot of luminosity appearing in the western sky shortly after sunset. In Richardson's script, the zodiacal light had suddenly attracted attention and was terrifying everyone, and Captain Video and the Rangers had been called upon to rectify the situation. Olga now commissioned me to visit Richardson in southern California and work over this script with him so that it became acceptable to use on television. I returned to Kenwood, then Norma and I drove south to Pacific Palisades, where Richardson had a beautiful house overlooking the ocean.

Richardson and I got along well together. He was about fifty years old, tall, spare, obviously intelligent, certainly no extrovert; in fact, he usually seemed detached and even rather moody. His wife Ursula was in complete contrast: she was considerably younger than he, blonde, carefully graceful, very elegant. Her brother was a notable Hollywood artist and something of the arty *avant-garde* mystique seemed part of Ursula's background. The topic of European travel came up; Ursula mentioned the Dolomites, Lake Como, the Riviera, all with wistful enthusiasm along with a rather reproachful glance toward Richardson, who had taken no great part in the conversation. When Ursula learned that Norma and I had just come back from a long stay in Europe, she became even more animated and turned Richardson a look of what almost seemed vindication. She said, "You see? This is how it can be done—these people know how to live!"

I explained our methods of travel, how Norma and I had come upon Stonehenge riding bicycles, and how we usually spent the night in bed-and-breakfast establishments. Ursula gave her head a jerk of disapproval and turned away; this was not the sort of travel she had in mind. She preferred the concepts of first-class and deluxe, and gay soirées into the small hours, Claridge's in London, the Ritz in Paris, and perhaps even a visit to Marienbad.

While we were living in Kenwood we made frequent expeditions to picturesque restaurants of the region. One such locale was Occidental, an old logging town, now deserted except for three magnificent restaurants: the Occidental, Fiore's, and the Union Hotel. Occidental was visited by folk from all over the bay area, and as far as I know, these three restaurants are still in business. Another of our favorite restaurants was located in a ghost town on the Sacramento River beside Walnut Grove. It consisted of dilapidated old structures which originally had been inhabited by gangs of Chinese laborers. Now there was nothing left except an antique shop and a restaurant known as Al the Wop's.

Upon entering Al the Wop's you found yourself in what was almost a caricature of the old-fashioned western saloon. The ceiling was covered with dollar bills, and it seemed that the patrons were encouraged to put thumbtacks through the dollar bills and fling them up at the ceiling. If the dollar bill stuck the patron received a free drink. The restaurant was at the back. The patron entered, seated himself, and a waitress came out and said, "Well done or rare?" The patron indicated his preference and the waitress went away. Presently the steak appeared, which of course was very good indeed.

Perhaps I should also mention Nepenthe, a beautiful restaurant in beautiful surroundings, situated on a bluff overlooking the ocean a few miles south of Big Sur. Our last visit was in the company of Ralph Vicinanza, my agent and good friend.

Volcano is a hamlet in the foothills of the Sierra Nevada mountains, and is not much except a few cottages and gas stations besides a local landmark known as Daffodil Hill. There is no volcano anywhere near, and in fact I have no idea how the place got its name. There is, however, an elegant resort hotel. On one occasion we organized a group of a dozen or so of our friends and set off on a junket to the Volcano hotel, where we would dine, spend the night, breakfast and return home. Present, as I recall, were Norma and myself, Poul Anderson and his wife Karen, Oscar Anderson, an electrical engineer and his wife Jedde, my nephew Stephen and his wife, Al Hall the guitar player, Bret Runkle, also an engineer, and Bret's wife Barbara, a beautiful blonde of Swedish extraction. After checking in we assembled in the bar. The sun was now definitely over the yardarm, and drinks began to flow in all directions, presaging a merry evening. Al Hall and another guitar player played some beautiful duets by Brazilian and Spanish composers. Elsewhere there was much laughing and joking and the exchanging of anecdotes.

After a while at the bar we moved into the dining room, where we dined on roast beef and *coq au vin*, drank wine, and congratulated ourselves upon our wisdom for being alive. Dessert was ice cream with coffee, then we rose from the table and circulated here and there. So far, the junket was proving a great success.

Poul and I found comfortable seats in the library, where we sat and thought serious thoughts, and theorized concerning the structure of the cosmos.

Now, at this time, I must draw a curtain of discretion over the subsequent events of the evening, which were rather tragic and destroyed a number of lives and affected many others, and I must be careful whose names I mention, since conceivably certain of these persons are still alive.

As Poul and I were sitting in the library, somebody I shall call Mr. X came up behind me and asked if he could use my car. Without thinking, I assented and handed him the key. He took it and went off, and I thought no more about it. An hour or so later, a great scandal hit the fan. It developed that Mr. X had induced another man's wife to drive off with him in my car and had not returned; in fact they did not return at all during the night, so that the next day Norma and I were forced to ride back to Oakland with Poul Anderson. Ultimately, I received my car back, but there were no apologies, merely a kind of bland fatalism. The event at Volcano had caused a great deal of damage which I will not trouble to particularize. I only bring it up here because it was a sad event which I often think about.

Richardson and I finally cobbled together a script which we thought might satisfy Olga Druce, who had changed the menace of the zodiacal light to the threat of an asteroid poised to strike earth. Later, Richardson took Norma and me up to the observatory, where we were privileged to look through the telescope. Then Norma and I returned north to Kenwood and resumed life as it had been before the Richardson collaboration.

Guests came and went, including the Hands, the Searses, Dick Oxtot and his first wife Joanne. We also saw a good deal of Frank Herbert and his wife Beverly, with whom we began formulating plans. Ultimately we decided upon a joint venture. We would set off to Mexico and set up a writers' household, and write Captain Video scripts and whatever else came to mind. To this end I traded in our Jeep for a Volkswagen station wagon, and the Herberts began selling off their possessions.

However, about this time, the Captain Video prospects went glimmering. On my last script or two, I had been letting my imagination range too far, injecting humor into the scripts and putting the characters into amusing predicaments. I got a call from Olga Druce complaining that I was turning Captain Video into a farce, and that my scripts would get her fired. Instead, she fired me.

Yet the Vances and the Herberts were not deterred from the Mexican project. We modified the VW station wagon to carry as much luggage as possible, but we were still faced with an impossibility. The luggage which Frank deemed indispensable was enough to load down a large truck—especially his stock of first-aid and medical equipment. Frank had allowed for every known disease and disability, from leprosy to six broken arms at once, for which contingency he had provided six slings. Beverly finally interceded and Frank's first-aid equipment was reduced to that which we could load aboard the VW.

Leaving Kenwood we drove south through California, across the border, down the west coast of Mexico, turned eastward to Guadalajara, then thirty miles further to Lake Chapala, which at that time had lost most of its water and was mainly mud flats. Here in Chapala we rented a very pleasant house a block or two from the main beer garden, which was always a source of amusement and entertainment, because musicians rolled through the place every night.

We set up our writers' workshop. We had an arrangement that when we hoisted a white flag, silence must descend upon the house, and nothing must occur that might disturb the writers, a system which worked out fairly well.

Life proceeded productively for a month or two. I don't know what Frank was writing; I wrote some short stories and started work on a novel which I called *Clarges* but which was ultimately published under the name *To Live Forever*, a title I detest. However, our income was less than our output, and in fact was nonexistent. Finally we were forced to terminate the writers' workshop and return to the States. Norma and I set off in our VW, but the Herberts relocated to San Miguel de Allende, where they remained for several more months.

Returning to the bay area, Norma and I began looking around for a place to settle. Eventually we came upon a spot in the Oakland hills, consisting of three lots and an old shack which we could rent with an option to buy. Since the price was right, we decided to buy and took steps to do so. At once we began rebuilding and expanding the shack, which entailed a great deal of digging out the hillside to give us a larger backyard. Over the years I must have moved a thousand wheelbarrows of dirt, maybe more.

The Herberts, coming back from Mexico, stopped by for a time, then continued north to Seattle. Frank said that they were planning to return to Mexico in due course, and in due course they did. On their way down from Seattle they stopped by to see us again, this time driving a hearse so loaded down with luggage that the fenders were scraping along the ground. Frank said that he planned to take the hearse down to San Miguel de Allende and have it converted into a station wagon. We did not hear from them for a while, but I don't think the conversion of the hearse to a station wagon was ever realized.

Somewhere about this time, wanderlust hit Norma and me again, and we embarked on another voyage. This time for a fact it was a voyage, aboard the Stromboli, a Liberty ship which, conceivably, I might have had some hand in building myself. We went aboard in Oakland and sailed south, stopping briefly in San Salvador. In order to go ashore, it was necessary to ride a flat-bottomed scow about twenty feet long, which upon reaching a dock was lifted out of the water by a crane and deposited on the dock. During our visit to San Salvador we had only enough time to visit the market and a few shops before returning to the Stromboli by means of the scow, which the crane politely dropped into the water. We passed through the Panama Canal, and eventually disembarked in Barcelona.

My mother, who had been traveling for some time, was now residing in the Oceano Hotel in Barcelona. We met her there, remained in Barcelona a few days, and the three of us took a ferry to Ibiza, where we rented a house. We chose Ibiza instead of Mallorca because our friends Gordon, Gwen and Tony were already established there. About a month later Gwen and Tony moved to the nearby island Formentera, where they built a house. I never saw it, and I can't imagine Tony building a house, but apparently he did. Gordon remained on Ibiza, where he met his girlfriend Vicki, whose home was in Madrid.

Every day I dived in the bay and collected stones. I put these in a sack and shipped them home, and ultimately they became paving for our front yard.

Our days in Ibiza passed pleasantly, although they encompassed very little social activity. Norma and my mother played bridge with another old couple while I spent most of my time writing or swimming down on the beach. A house nearby was inhabited by an Australian painter and his wife, whom I got to know to some extent. He was tall, gaunt, rather odd-looking, with a habit of speaking with his eyes focused on the horizon.

Five years later or so, in Australia, I thought I would look him up. I did, and discovered that he was a famous artist in his own country. I went to visit him at his house, rang the door. He opened the door, looked at me with a look of mild inquiry—but evidently no recognition—on his face.

"I'm Jack," I said awkwardly. "We were neighbors on Ibiza."

"Oh, yes," he said. "That was a long time ago. Well, it was nice to have seen you again. Goodbye."

And that was that.

In Ibiza we patronized two bars; one was "Dirty Juan" and the other was "Clean Juan." Dirty Juan was the closest, and that was the one we used most often. Gordon related an incident that occurred one night when he and some of the other regulars decided to try some psychokinesis or table-raising, by laying hands flat on the table and making it move. Gordon swore to me, backwards and forwards, his eyes bulging blue and earnest, that the table jerked, jumped and started up toward the ceiling.

One evening Gordon hosted a party which was attended by a dozen or so, maybe more, local people and tourists, most of whom I did not know. It was a jolly party; I had my cornet with me. There was also a guitar player on hand who knew the chords to some of the tunes which happened to be in my own repertoire, so we began playing together. We were doing pretty well, but after about five minutes a young fellow nearby said, "Let me play." I told him no, but he insisted. "I want to play— let me play!" I said that I had not brought my cornet miles and miles across the ocean for him to play, I had brought it for me to play. At that he got rather hostile and picked a fistfight with me. Gordon interceded before any harm was done. I learned from this episode that a musical instrument would seem to be a dangerous thing to carry with you while you were traveling; there's no telling where the thing may lead you.

Ibiza was and no doubt is a pleasant place, although I am sorry that we were never able to visit Mallorca, which is supposedly one of the most picturesque of all the Spanish islands.

In due course we took our leave. We ferried to Barcelona, went by train to Andorra, and thence into France. We separated from my mother, who went off into Germany, while we proceeded to Geneva where Red Sears and his wife were in residence and studying child psychiatry under the famous Piaget.

Gordon, Gwen and Tony and I had arranged to meet in Morocco, so Norma and I set out to the south on a train, which took us through Spain to Gibraltar, where we ferried across to Tangiers. In Tangiers we had our first experience with the Moroccan *souk*, which is a warren of alleys and pathways and hundreds of little stalls where brasses, carvings, fabrics and much else were sold. The outlander entering the *souk* needed a guide, otherwise he would become lost. This was the case with all the other *souks* we visited in Morocco.

From Tangiers we took a bus to Fez, where we met our friends. After a time Norma and I set off south to Marrakesh and established ourselves in a French hotel. Marrakesh is famous for its *Djemaa el Fna*, the main square and marketplace of the city's old quarter. Here locals and tourists may find fruits and vegetables, colorful clothing, trained monkeys, snake-charmers, storytellers, magicians, singers, dancers, peddlers of every sort— and of course all manner of food, purveyed by cooks yammering from stalls crowded shoulder-to-shoulder. Norma and I spent an afternoon on a terrace, drinking beer and overlooking the *Djemaa el Fna*, marveling at what we saw.

Leaving Marrakesh, we took a bus to the east and up through the Atlas Mountains, to a town called Ksar es Souk,[11] where we spent the night. That evening we visited a bar, where a group of French legionnaires sat drinking beer inexplicably colored dark pink and green. Norma and I were puzzled but ultimately discovered that the soldiers had mixed their beer with liqueurs of various sorts to produce these unlikely colors.

---

11. Now Er Rachidia.

The next day the bus dropped down the eastern slopes of the Atlas and took us into the Sahara to Erfoud, a little oasis town where the French National Railway had constructed a remarkable luxury hotel. We registered at this hotel and found ourselves to be the solitary guests.

Gordon, Gwen and Tony joined us at the hotel. We spent a rollicking evening and the next day explored the little village beside the oasis. After a day or two we returned to Marrakesh, and here we parted. Gordon, Gwen and Tony returned to Spain; Norma and I continued on to Casablanca, and south to Agadir, which I thought might communicate with the Canary Islands. This is a famous route, along which goats climb the argan trees to graze on the leaves.

At Agadir we found that there was no direct passage to the Canary Islands, so we spent the night in a hotel. On this evening occurred a strange event. Norma and I both ordered turkey for our supper. The waiter was a tall sardonic Frenchman. Norma received a generous plate of turkey with all the trimmings. I in turn received a plate upon which was nothing but a scrawny drumstick, hard as a rock and as inedible. I was outraged at this apparent insult, naturally, and tried to summon the waiter, but he only turned his back and walked away after sparing me a leer of contempt. I should have called for the manager, but we simply left.

The following day we returned to Casablanca, where we took a ship to the Canary Islands. We landed in Tenerife and spent the night in a hotel, regarding which I remember little other than the supper we were served there. This was a liver stew, which turned out to be quite palatable. The next day we ferried to Gran Canaria. Here, after a certain amount of investigation, we discovered *La Solana*, a house about fifteen miles south of Las Palmas. *La Solana* was notable because the previous tenants, Americans, had written a book about the place. We read this book, and everything they had written about their surroundings we could apply to ourselves.

We spent a pleasant two months at *La Solana*. I wrote and practiced my cornet; we dined upon the meals provided by Carmela, the cook we had hired.

In the museum of Las Palmas, to my great surprise, I came upon a set of paintings produced by the artist-in-residence entitled *Poem of Atlantis*. By coincidence I had previously discovered these pictures reproduced in an art book and had pasted them into my scrapbook.

In due course we left the Canaries, returned to Casablanca and flew to Dakkar, where we boarded the train which was to take us to Timbuktu.

Along the way we encountered a plague of locusts which flew into the window and permeated the car, giving Norma a great fright; ever after she became squeamish at the word "locust." We arrived at a town called Bamako, and as we spent the night in the hotel I took stock of our finances. We had $1,800, which at the time was enough to get us to Timbuktu and across to the east coast of Africa one way or another…but then what? On the other hand, it was enough to get us back home. And since I had not received any money in the mail, and had no immediate prospects of receiving any, I began envisioning Norma and I stranded at Timbuktu, sitting in the market square, singing and dancing and holding out alms bowls. We cowered, turned around the next day, Timbuktu at our backs, a dream-place we would never visit. We returned to Dakkar, boarded an airplane to Lisbon and another back to our safe, snug home in California where again we kissed the ground and gave thanks to the spirits which inhabited eucalyptus trees.

The next situation of any consequence, aside from our activities working on the house, making improvements, throwing what remained of the old shack out the window, was the birth of our son John, which of course was the preeminent event of our lives so far. It was 1961.

John was a nice baby. He never yelled, or at least never to excess. When he was four years old he would dry the dishes while I washed, and I taught him multiplication tables while we did the dishes. Being an awfully smart kid, he learned them instantly.

During these times I did a lot of writing—besides working on the house, as always—and we had parties. Many of these were musical parties. I took Tony Boucher to a jam session one night; he was much impressed, never having been to any such occasion before. I saw a great deal of Poul Anderson. He and I used to go out once a week or so to have lunch, and these occasions were always pleasant. I met Al Hall the guitarist. There have been two Al Halls in my life: one played piano and trombone, and the other guitar. This latter is still alive and lives in Mendocino and we are still in touch.

Eventually, the little wander-bug began biting again, and at a point when I had sold something to make a little money, and when there seemed to be more money in the offing, Norma and I decided to take a trip in a different direction: namely, to the west. This time it was Tahiti that beckoned.

Preparations were made; and one day in 1965 we set off.

"I teie nie mahana
Ne tere no oe e Hati
Na te Moana!"
*"Let us sing and make merry,
For we journey over the sea!"*
—Tahitian festal song

CHAPTER 7

WE ARRIVED AT the Faaa's International Airport, three miles southwest of Papeete, and for the first day or so put up in a rather run-down hotel. A few days later we came upon a house for rent in the district known as Paea, near the beach about twelve miles east of Papeete. The house itself was plain but nicely furnished, and the setting was almost too perfect to be true. Next door was a Chinese grocery, where beautiful loaves of French bread sold for 10¢ apiece, and the beach was fifty yards away. We also had access to a dugout canoe.

We settled in, set up housekeeping, and began to churn out fiction. These were absolutely idyllic circumstances. Along the driveway were pineapple bushes, although I don't think we ever harvested any pineapple. In the backyard was a lime tree full of fruit, in the front a custard apple tree, which dropped custard apples on the roof of our house, which always made a thunderous bang. For supplies unavailable at the Chinese grocery, Norma rode the bus into Papeete and then back, which was no great ordeal. The Tahitian ladies doted upon Johnny. Our beach fronted on the lagoon, and I usually went swimming every day. I tried to teach Johnny to swim; he wasn't quite ready for it, but he liked to dabble around in the water. Norma found a place where the tides left shells, and she formed a daily habit of going out and combing the shore for beautiful shells.

We received news of an unfortunate occurrence back in New York. One of Scott Meredith's associates sold one of my stories to Frederick Pohl, who was currently editor of *Galaxy* magazine, but then unwittingly sold the same story to another publication. This meant that Fred Pohl could not use the story and there was all hell to pay. Scott Meredith fired the guilty associate, but no one made any move to reimburse me, so I simply gritted my teeth and sat down to write another story for Fred. This became *The Last Castle*, which turned out to be a pretty good story.

Cannibalism was never practiced on Tahiti—at least so I am told, although it was once common practice among the Marquesas. At one time Tahiti was divided into a dozen or so districts, each inhabited by a tribe, often at war with its neighbor. When a member of one tribe ventured into the center of the island in order to hunt wild pig, and came upon a warrior from another tribe, he had to make a choice: they could either fight, or one of them could hold up his hands in a sort of salute, and say: "Iorana!" which means, "I give you your life." The other would shout back the same phrase, then the two would perhaps bow to each other and continue hunting for wild pig.

One day I joined Norma on a shopping trip into Papeete. When the shopping was accomplished we had lunch in a Chinese restaurant, which was much like Chinese restaurants everywhere else in the world. Norma visited the restroom, and when she returned she reported that a sign hung in the stall saying: "YOU ARE BEING WATCHED! THROW NOTHING IN THE TOILET!"

As we rode back to Paea, aboard the bus I thought to refresh myself and pulled the top off a can of beer. A middle-aged man was sitting on the bench across from us. He looked nervously toward the driver, then shook his head at me. He said, "Stow that beer—if the cops see you, they'll throw you in jail."

As I recall, I continued to drink the beer, but surreptitiously, with guilty looks in all directions, and I got talking to the gentleman who had warned us. So I found out later, he was no gentleman; he was a scalawag and a beachcomber named Alf Kinander. He got off the bus in Paea as we did, and I invited him into the house, and there we had some beer legitimately. Alf lived in a house not far inland. He was married to a Tahitian lady and they had five daughters, two of whom were married to American lawyers.

During our stay in Tahiti, Alf Kinander and I saw much of each other, and I became attached to him. He had wonderful tales to tell, some of them not altogether credible, but always entertaining. His daughters, so he reported, had joined the Mormon church. I asked why on earth the Mormons. He said because the Mormons will walk the girls home; if they walk home by themselves, someone will rape them. I thought, well, that seemed as good a reason as any to be a Mormon.

Kinander told me of haunted places and of witches, and of one witch in particular who had placed a curse upon him and who, he claimed, was causing him many small misfortunes. Alf at last confronted the witch and, threatening severe consequences, induced her to lay off her mischief. That brought and end to the witchery, according to Kinander.

Kinander's youngest daughter, Bernice, was at this time three years old. Every year in July the Tahitians celebrate a French holiday and for a week there are all manner of festivities and dances and contests and great to-do. Many years after we had left Tahiti, I chanced upon an account of the year's celebration in Tahiti, where it was announced that the beauty queen of Tahiti was Bernice Kinander.

Several cottages away there lived a Cliff Katz. He was caretaker for a big barkentine anchored in the lagoon. I went out with him one day and looked over this barkentine; very impressive it was.

We had several parties during our stay in Tahiti. At one of them, Cliff Katz and his sixteen-year-old daughter Hinano were on hand. As always, Hinano looked extremely cute, and her looks were enhanced by a little black hat she wore with a feather in it.[12] As Al Hall, who was visiting us, played the guitar, Cliff and Hinano danced, and it must be said that the Tahitian dance is a rather grotesque one, with the males performing one sort of antic and the females another.

We had become friendly with our landlord, a middle-aged Tahitian with a large family, and one day we invited him to one our parties. At the appointed hour on the appointed day, a bus pulled into the driveway loaded with our landlord's relatives, many playing guitars and singing, and with a big barrelful of ice and beer in the center of the bus. In my long checkered career I have participated in many parties of many sorts, but this was the most remarkable of my lifetime. There has never been anything like it.

In Papeete there was a dance hall and saloon known as Quinn's. It dated back to 1860 and was originally Quinn's Ice Cream Parlor, and was known far and wide across the Pacific. In fact, Quinn's was legendary. At one point it stopped being an ice cream parlor and became a cabaret. While Al Hall was in Tahiti, we visited Quinn's twice. The second time we were there, we were sitting at a table and talking to two or three French legionnaires. The room was crowded with dancing people. While we were talking to these two we looked away for a moment; when we looked back one of them was missing. We looked around

---

12. The Tahitian word *Hinano* has multiple meanings. It is first the name of a flower, the lovely bloom of the *hala* tree or screwpine, *Pandanus odoratissimus*. Second, it is the name of Tahiti's most popular beer, the label of which is a work of art. Third, *Hinano* is a girl's name—notably, Hinano Katz, whom I have mentioned. Fourth, it is the name that Johnny and I subsequently applied to our 45-foot ketch, which still plies San Francisco Bay.

and saw that he was down on the floor. Somebody had knocked him off his feet. He got back up, looked around the dance floor, but could not determine who had performed this quiet deed. He stood there a while, shrugged, turned back and we continued our discussion. At some point we chanced to look away again, and once more the soldier fell to the floor, clouted by the same unseen assailant. He again picked himself up and looked around, but as before could not identify the perpetrator. We never did learn anything further; this particular soldier moved around the other side of the table, so that he was safe from further attacks.

Al Hall returned to the States, and the house in Paea became rather lonely. One day Johnny wandered down the beach to play with his friends, and after an hour or so came wandering back. Some unknown individual had given him a fine haircut, pomaded his hair and combed it. It was as if this person, seeing this kid with the straggly hair, couldn't bear the sight, and threw him into a barber's chair.

I finished writing whatever I was working on, and Norma and I decided that it was time to move on. It was hard to do so, since we had formed attachments to our friends Kinander and Katz, and to our landlord, and some Tahitians who lived across the street and with whom we had become acquainted. There was also a little girl named Fairo, who played every day with Johnny, and we had to say goodbye to her as well. The bus took us to the Faaa Airport, where we boarded a plane and set off to Australia.

Twenty or thirty years later, Johnny and I had visited Australia to attend a science-fiction convention at which I was guest of honor. On our way home we stopped off in Tahiti to visit our friend Hayford Peirce, who lived there. We discovered to our consternation that Quinn's, the legendary bar, had been torn down and replaced with a boutique or something equally frivolous. All right-thinking men regard this act as sacrilege. As far as I was concerned Quinn's was the only landmark in the whole south Pacific of any significance, not counting perhaps Easter Island.

Upon sober reflection, I feel that I must amend the above remark. There is another landmark in the South Pacific. It is on the island Mangareva, where a mad priest dragooned the population of the island to build an enormous cathedral, at the cost of how many lives I don't know. The cathedral stands today on this forlorn island out to the east of Tahiti.

Allow me to be discursive for a moment or two, because Mangareva is an interesting place. A few years back it was visited by a young anthropologist who wished to perform research upon the nature of the inhabitants. On a small nearby island he discovered that the ancient indigenes had dug tunnels into the mountainside, for what purpose he could not divine, but he proposed to find out. It appears that he was a man of good physique, about five-foot-ten inches tall, broad-shouldered, but the tunnels had been built by a race of people who in general were considerably smaller than himself. As I contemplate his activity, which occurred many years ago and many thousands of miles away, I can't help to marvel at his audacity. I shudder when I think of the claustrophobia. In any event, he made his way along these tunnels down into the mountains, finding nothing, and finally came to a place where the tunnel curved sharply upward. He found himself unable to move forward and that the tunnel was too narrow to allow him to turn around. I forget now how he contrived to save himself, but he did by one means or another. I don't want to be an anthropologist if it means exploring ancient tunnels.

One more word about Mangareva. I have a book here by a man who went to live on Mangareva for a time. He inhabited a cottage beside a waterway. It seemed a pleasant place under the palm trees, but for some reason he found himself uncomfortable in this cottage. He was uneasy, could not sleep well, had bad dreams, was constantly nervous and looking over his shoulder. One day he mentioned his disquietude to a friend, who laughed and said, "Your disquiet is easily explained: you are living beside the area where the war canoes would return with captives and take them out and kill them, right beside your front door." The gentleman moved to a new cottage, and immediately his fears and discomforts came to an end, and the bad dreams were a thing of the past.

Upon leaving Tahiti we flew to Australia, but I am not going to dwell too long on this particular trip. We met Bertram Chandler, the writer, and we moved into an apartment on Bondi Beach close to the water. Bondi Beach is protected from sharks by a net a hundred yards out to sea. John was happy to play out in the sand, where he buried and lost the toy truck he had been given for his fourth birthday. Norma became ill; she went to the hospital and was diagnosed with hepatitis.

In due course we all returned to California and life resumed. That first venture into Australia was not a success, but there would be others far more satisfactory.

At home, life proceeded along familiar patterns. I worked on the house; Norma and I produced fiction. John and I dug in the hillside, thereby widening our backyard. When I think about it now, I am amazed by the amount of dirt John and I moved.

At this time I embarked on a new project: I decided to build a houseboat. With great care I drew up the plans. The houseboat would float on two pontoons, each 32 feet long. There would be a forward deck about four feet wide, a control cabin, a main room, a bathroom and a back porch.

Frank Herbert had moved down from Seattle and was now working on a newspaper in San Francisco. Frank and

Poul Anderson decided to become partners in the houseboat venture. I build the pontoons in our front yard out of plywood, and I fiberglassed them carefully. When they were completed, we transported them by truck out to a marina around the bay at Point Molate, where they were to be launched into the water.

Now I committed an egregious blunder. If I had thought about it, I could have very easily launched these pontoons single-handedly, by laying out planks and rollers and pushing the pontoons into the water. Instead I had to make a party of it, inviting many of my friends out to this beach, where I thought we would simply lift the pontoons and carry them into the water. For a time I had been deliberating as to how this should best be done, then someone—I forget who it was—became bored with my apparent indecision, and said, "Come on, let's get these things in the water!" He and some others ran down, took the pontoons and dragged them—without lifting them—across the gravel-strewn beach and into the water. In the process they tore the fiberglass off the bottom of one of the pontoons. The other escaped unharmed.

In any event, there were the two pontoons floating in the water. We floated them out around the piers to the berth where the construction of the house would proceed. There the day ended.

Over the weeks that followed, Poul, Frank and I built the house. Most of the work fell on my shoulders, naturally, since Frank was forced to come over from San Francisco, and Poul was not a carpenter.

The project had reached its final stages, and then one night disaster struck down from the sky. First a big storm blew in, and sent big waves crashing. At the same time the worms finally broke through the pontoon where the fiberglass had been scraped off, the pontoon filled with water, and the houseboat sank. I received a telephone call to the effect that the houseboat had gone under. When we arrived, we saw one corner of the houseboat sticking up out of the water and were, needless to say, dismayed.

When the storm ended we surveyed the damage. Frank had had enough. He exited the program; he wanted nothing to do with a sunken houseboat. Poul and I were left to raise it ourselves. Poul could not enter the water because of ear problems, therefore it fell to me, Bill the Lizard.

My nephew Steve assisted us in the operation. We took an air compressor out and eight fifty-gallon drums. I climbed into a wet suit and jumped into the water, and there, by careful manipulation—first filling the drums with water and guiding them under the houseboat, fixing them at the proper places, then pumping air into them from the compressor—the houseboat rose to the surface. We were thrilled by our victory over the elements! By now, if for no other reason, I gained a full and total respect for Poul Anderson, who had shown himself a truly staunch human being. I won't say any more about Poul, except that to this day I think of him often.

We towed the houseboat to the beach, raised it up so that we could get at the pontoon, which we repaired. We moved the houseboat back in the water and completed the construction.

Al Hall became the third partner, taking Frank Herbert's place. At last the houseboat was ready to be moved to its ultimate destination.

The Mokelumne River joins the San Joaquin River in the delta, and along the shore are a number of marinas. At one of these marinas we found a convenient berth. One morning we set out from Point Richmond, proceeding across the bay. We were powered by a 25-horsepower outboard engine, which pushed us at about five or six knots. We crossed under the Carquinez Bridge, proceeded up the river, and turned into what was known as the Big Break, near Oakley, where at one time floodwaters had burst through the levees and created a lake. Here we anchored for the night.

The next day we continued to our berth and moored there, safe and sound, ready to use the houseboat.

I may say in passing that Erle Stanley Gardner, the great mystery novelist, also had a houseboat, not in our marina but somewhat north near the town of Walnut Grove.

Every week or so we would drive up on Friday afternoon, board the boat, fill the tank with water, the gas tank with gas, put out from the marina and make our way down to some pleasant spot, perhaps on the Big Break where we could look out over the water, drop anchor, and there—well, the men would sit on the front porch drinking beer, while the ladies whomped up dinner on the inside. We also took friends with us, and once or twice Frank Herbert joined us, looking over the situation.

A single problem evolved on the houseboat: it was difficult to manage in a strong wind. One afternoon we took the houseboat several miles upriver, and there a ferocious wind came up from the north. We turned back, but found that it was impossible to steer in a straight course. The wind pushed us sideways down the river. Nevertheless, by dint of painstaking seamanship, we managed to get the houseboat back into the marina, in the process of which Al Hall fell overboard. Thus we learned that it was not a good idea to venture out when the wind was blowing.

On another occasion Norma and I and John went up and anchored for the night, as usual, near the Big Break. In the morning, when we awoke, we found that a dense fog had settled over the area, so we could not see ten feet ahead of us. We wanted to return to the berth, so now some expert navigation was required. As I recall, it was a very eerie experience, navigating through the fog trying to locate landmarks. But eventually we succeeded, returned to our berth, congratulated ourselves, kissed the ground and went home.

The years passed. Norma and I worked on our house, produced fiction, occasionally visited the houseboat, but not as often as before. Then, about 1968 or '69, certain things happened—Poul became ill and was no longer able to join us on the houseboat, and Al Hall was transferred north to Mendocino so that I was alone in possession of the houseboat. Norma and I were once again prosperous and, as in the past whenever this had occurred, we were thinking of far-off places with sweet-sounding names. So I gave the houseboat to Ali Szantho, who was trying to organize a professional soccer league without any particular success. I never found out what happened later, but Ali hinted that he had incurred a misfortune. He had run the houseboat into some rocks along the shore, and the houseboat was no more. So ended the era of the magnificent houseboat.

And in the vats of Luna
This year, the must shall foam
Round the feet of laughing girls
Whose sires have marched to Rome.
—Thomas Babington Macaulay

CHAPTER 8

OUR OLD WANDERLUST, which seemed to come upon us every several years, struck again in the 1969.

We put our house in the care of friends and set off to the east coast. We loaded the VW aboard the oceanliner *France*, and climbed aboard third class. The cuisine on the *France* fell short of our expectations, and the wine served with our meals was the most fearful swill I have ever imbibed. The French ought to have been ashamed of themselves.

We disembarked at Southampton and drove west through Devon and down to Land's End at the southwestern tip of Cornwall. The British use a phrase: "From Land's End to John o' Groats," which describes the longest distance one can travel in Great Britain, over 600 miles from southwest to northeast. John o' Groats, incidentally, is a town named for a Dutchman, Jan de Groot, who in the 15th century established a ferry plying between Scotland and the Orkney Islands.

From Land's End we drove north, through the Lorna Doone country and Waters Meet, through Shropshire, Northamptonshire, Yorkshire and into Scotland. We spent two days in Edinburgh, where we climbed up Edinburgh Rock and explored Edinburgh Castle, a majestic structure which over-looks the city.

In a local haberdashery we bought two duffel coats, one for Norma and one for John. These were heavy blue garments equipped with hoods which protect the wearer from the high winds and unpredictable weather of Scotland. Later, everywhere we traveled, we collected decorative patches, which we sewed upon John's duffel coat until it was quite wonderfully bedizened.

We continued north into Inverness, past Loch Ness, where John, investigating the surface of the lake, declared that he had seen Nessie. Norma and I strained to see her ourselves, but without success.

Eventually we arrived at John o' Groats, which wasn't much of anything but a desolate old inn, where we spent the night. Thus we gratified our need to realize the ancient English proverb. From Land's End to John o' Groats—there we were.

The next day we set off westward, past the peninsula Tongue, which Gordon Tongue claimed to be the home of his ancestors, and toward Cape Wrath, which I had hoped to visit. However, we found that there was a body of water intervening, and the ferries were no longer in operation. So we turned south, driving along the coast, through Sutherland, and the area where theoreti-cally would be situated Lochdubh, the locale of M. C. Beaton's mystery series detailing the exploits of Hamish Macbeth.

We passed through Inverness and stopped for the night at an inn, where we heard for the first time the music of Jimmy Shand and his orchestra. I will take this occasion to remark on this music, which at the time was popular in Scotland and Ireland. I am not sure as to the instrumentation of Shand's band—there certainly were several strings, accordion, drums, piano, bass, perhaps clarinet. The music is hard to describe; it certainly was not what you would call pop music—there were no vocals—but it was evidently based upon traditional Scottish themes or courtly Scottish dances and marches. It had a unique lilt, and

I have never come upon anyone who has heard this music and has not been charmed by it.

A day or two later we ferried across the Minch to the Isle of Skye. We spent the night at an inn in Portree, the island's largest settlement. The next day we drove around the island, through a dramatically beautiful landscape of hills and mists and shadows. In the evening we arrived at Camasunary on the Strathaird peninsula, and took lodging for the night at a nearby inn.[13]

We dined on fish and chips, then went into the lounge. I noticed that the clerk at the registration desk was idly plucking a guitar. In the lounge we were served beer and sat by the fire. Five or ten minutes later, three men came into the lounge. One was carrying an accordion, the other two fiddle cases. From behind the registration desk came the young man with his guitar. The fiddlers brought forth their instruments; they all tuned up and began to play music in more or less the same style of the Jimmy Shand repertoire.

While the group was playing, a middle-aged man and his wife entered the lounge. The lady was a comfortable matron, the man short, sandy-haired, and wearing a black suit, which was obviously not his everyday wear. As they entered, one of them cried out, "Angus, you're here at last! Yonder are the pipes, come join us now for a tune."

Angus smiled and shook his head, "No, it would nae be proper. We have just come from the funeral of old Wooter McKenna, and it would nae be seemly to play the pipes."

"Not so!" cried the younger musician. "Old Wooter'd take joy in the music! Come now, let's have a tune to send old Wooter's ghost hoppin' and skippin' away."

Angus turned his head sideways and pursed his lips; he looked at his wife. She shrugged, and Angus said, "Well, I

---

13. Camasunary, incidentally, is the setting for Mary Stewart's novel *Wildfire at Midnight*, one of her most suspenseful murder mysteries.

suppose a tune might be reverential. I can play with a reverential soul for the sake of old Wooter. Where are the pipes?"

The pipes were handed to Angus; the music began, and it was the most beautiful music to be heard anywhere. Angus, however, would only play one reverential tune; then he gave up the pipes and he and his wife settled down beside the fire with pints of ale.

On the next day we left Skye, drove down the coast and took the ferry to Ireland. We landed in Belfast, and on the next day drove south to Dublin, where we spent two or three days seeing the sights. Leaving Dublin we drove west across Ireland to Cong, and lodged ourselves in Ashford Castle on the shores of Lough Corrib (or Loch Coirib in Irish). In the morning we learned of a cottage which might be rented a few miles to the west beside the lake. Taking ourselves to this cottage we met the owners, the Molloys, examined their cottage, and promptly rented it.

We subsequently became friendly with the Molloys. Jackie Molloy worked in the forest; Mary Molloy kept house at home. There were three children: Kathleen and Maureen, girls about John's age, and Sean, a little younger. At a pier on the lake was moored a rowboat, which we were entitled to use. Upshore was the island Inchagoill, where some of the local farmers took their cattle and let them rove free. Another island four or five miles away had been the resort of medieval monks, and the site of an ancient cemetery and a chapel rumored to have been visited by St. Patrick during the Middle Ages.

Norma and I settled down to work, and occasionally gave John instruction in the schoolwork he was missing. These prolonged absences from school never seemed to cause John any difficulty. On returning home, he always rejoined his classes as if he had never been away.

In the cottage there were two bedrooms, a living room, kitchen and bathroom. In the living room was a fireplace where we burned turf, which produces a fine fire. The turf is created by a man who carries a spadelike instrument known as a slane. He goes to the bog, digs out long slabs of the wet material which he lays out to dry along the bank. Presently, the wet stuff dries and becomes turf. It burns slowly, giving off a wonderful resinous odor which will bring heartsickness and longing to any Irishman.

The climate was fickle and changeable. The day would start out with sun, then there would be a spat of rain, then clouds, then maybe a touch of sleet or snow, then more sun, more rain… Mind you, this was winter. Yet the cold never became severe.

During the summer, the Molloys rented the cottage to fishermen, who caught trout in the lake. Johnny and I often used the boat; I rowed back and forth while Johnny fished. We never got so much as a bite, but nobody had told us that during the winter the fish refused to cooperate with the fisherman. Still, it was fun and good exercise. The lakewater was a peculiar dark brown, almost black, and sometimes reefs of rock would almost reach the surface, and a boat with any draft at all would find itself in trouble. However, we managed to avoid these reefs.

We bought groceries in Cong, and once a week drove south to Galway for meat and other goods not available in Cong. In olden times, as a traveler entered Galway, he passed under a massive stone arch, into which was chiseled a devout and dire supplication:

FROM THE SAVAGE DEEDS OF THE O'FLAHERTYS
MAY THE GOOD LORD PROTECT US!

We found Galway to be a rather strange city. On one occasion, we went into a bank to cash a cheque for $1,000. Without comment, and without even asking for identification, the manager handed us the money in Irish pounds. Even in 1969, such a transaction would have been unthinkable in the United States!

On another occasion, we stopped to lunch in a restaurant. One of the waitresses approached with pad and pencil to take our order, but at this moment a fat young priest wearing his clerical robes entered the restaurant and seated himself at a nearby table. Instantly, our waitress abandoned us and ran over to attend his needs, as did two or three other waitresses. We waited and waited. Meanwhile, the waitresses brought out a platter upon which rested a beautifully cooked fish, and set this before the priest, together with all the trimmings. The priest smiled benevolently; he uttered no blessings, nor did he make any ecclesiastical gestures, but raising his elbows tucked into the fish. Finally our waitress, with nothing else to do, deigned to take our order.

Near the cottage lived Reggie McNab, a cousin of the Molloys who, together with his wife, operated a small grocery in Cong. One evening we invited the McNabs and the Molloys to dinner. Norma served a curry of beef with garnishes of chutney and toasted coconut, with apple pie with cheese for dessert. By Norma's standards it was a pleasant but not notably dramatic meal.

Several weeks later, Norma visited the McNabs' shop in Cong but found little to inspire her; eventually she settled on a couple of undersized, wrinkled tomatoes. These she took to the counter, where Mrs. McNab stood at the cash register. Mrs. McNab looked at the tomatoes, then at Norma, and said: "Still eatin' high, Mrs. Vance?"

Christmas arrived. Jackie Molloy, who worked as a forester, brought us a small tree, and Norma fashioned a set of ornaments from tin cans, which we hung on the tree. We have these ornaments to this day and they still hang on our tree every Christmas.

We seldom strayed far from our cottage. One day we drove south to the cliffs of Moher, which are spectacular. They run south along the ocean for miles, rising five hundred feet sheer above the water. Another day we drove north to Donegal, Yeats country. But for the most part we remained in our cottage, working hard, producing fiction, and occasionally rowing on the lake.

One evening Jackie Molloy and I went into the nearby town of Cornamona and looked up one of Jackie's friends. He took us into his barn, and there took Jackie aside into an earnest colloquy, the meanwhile glancing at me over their shoulders and making odd signals to one another. When Jackie's friend was at last assured that I could be trusted, he sold me a bottle of the Irish white lightning, *poteen*, falsely labeled for whisky. Jackie and I returned to the cottage and there sampled the contents, which indeed had both character and authority.

One January day Norma, Johnny and I went for a drive in the country. The weather had been cold for Ireland and the roads were slick with ice. Ahead of us a truck was parked in the road. I braked hard, but the tires skidded on the ice and we slid into the back of the truck. The front of the car was damaged but otherwise nothing serious happened. Nevertheless, we were all shaken up. We might have had the damage repaired locally, but I did not trust Irish mechanics, and since we were now ready to depart Ireland, we decided to take the car to a VW agency in Germany and have the repairs done by experts.

We said goodbye to the Molloys, took off, drove through Ireland to the south coast. Along the way we stopped in Cork and bought several settings of Belleek dinnerware, and at the Waterford Works a crystal chandelier, which to this day hangs in our dining room.

At Rosslare Harbour at the southeastern corner of Ireland we boarded a steamferry, which took us directly to Cherbourg on the coast of France, bypassing England. From Cherbourg we drove northeast to Aachen, the spa-city on the north Rhine and onetime seat of Charlemagne. We took lodging in a pleasant little hotel at the edge of town, beside a small fountain. Once situated, we took our car to the local VW garage.

During this stopover in Aachen, Johnny met with a memorable experience. Not far from the hotel lived a crotchety old man who was forever victimized by the naughty boys of the neighborhood. They sassed and taunted him mercilessly, and generally made his life miserable. One day Johnny was innocently sailing his boat in the fountain. The old man happened to be in the vicinity, and must have identified Johnny with his tormentors, for he came up behind Johnny, seized him, and gave him a vigorous spanking. The spanking startled Johnny more than physically hurt him; in any case he was not amused by the incident.

In due course we returned to the garage to pick up our car. The office at the garage was dominated by an enormous computer, primitive and cumbersome by today's standards, and perhaps even by those of the day. The clerk used this machine to calculate our bill. He inserted card after card into a slot, and the computer whirred and whined, processing the information on the cards, finally compiling our grand total. If the mechanic put so much as a dab of Vaseline on a piece of metal, he wrote out a card saying "Dab of Vaseline" and the computer reckoned this on the bill. When the full reckoning was at last presented to us, we were taken aback. It was staggering. Yet with no other option, we paid the balance and went off with our car, only to discover that the job had been only half-done. The front fenders were still dented, and furthermore patched with gray primer instead of properly painted. I should mention that our car was red. Yet we dared not return and give the computer a second foray into our checkbook, so on we went. In hindsight, my advice to anyone who owns a Volkswagen is: If it needs repairs, do not take it to a German garage.

We learned that our friends Gordon Tongue, Gwen and Tony were now residing in Torremolinos, on the Costa del Sol on the southern coast of Spain. We decided to join them there.

Departing Aachen, we drove south through France, stopping at small inns and resorts recommended by the Michelin travel guides. These Michelin guides, incidentally, are invaluable for persons traveling through Great Britain, France, Italy, Germany and perhaps elsewhere. Restaurants and hotels are rated with extreme care and vigilance, and at this time there were perhaps fewer than ten restaurants in France with a three-star rating. The symbol of a small black rocking chair in the guide indicated a desirable place of lodging. When such a place was particularly charming and comfortable, the rocking chair would be red. We found that a red rocking chair usually indicated an inexpensive if high-quality country inn, situated in romantic surroundings, which also took pride in its cuisine. These little inns were favored by thrifty Frenchmen on their holidays, and they also became the same for us. We traveled through France from one red rocking chair to another.

Several years earlier, at Poul Anderson's house in Orinda, we had been introduced to François Bordes, an eminent French archeologist. We now visited him at his home in Bordeaux. He graciously showed us many implements from the Stone Age, and then took us out to dine at a restaurant nearby. During the meal I was served a little pot full of little things that looked like worms swimming in tomato sauce. Not wishing to appear gauche I ate these things, only to learn afterwards that that they were baby eels. I consider myself a brave man.

We spent several days at Les Eyzies, where Norma and John visited the famous Cro-Magnon caves. I, however, remained in our lodging that day with a cold.

Leaving Les Eyzies we continued south through Biarritz and into Spain, then westward along the coast road, which at that time was two-laned, and crammed with trucks moving at no great speed. If this road is now as it was then, it cannot be recommended as a scenic route.

We stopped at Altamira, the site of another cave decorated with paleolithic art. On this occasion I was able to join Norma and John, and the three of us explored the cave together and marveled at the wall-paintings. We spent the night at a nearby *parador*, one of the many splendid government-managed hotels that usually occupy an old castle or building of some significance.

Eventually we found a road leading south and in due course arrive in Portugal—a country which I hold in high esteem, and whose cuisine, though not fancy nor in any way spectacular, is simply excellent.

We celebrated John's eighth birthday in the enormous Buçaco Palace Hotel, then turned to the east and once more into Spain, ultimately arriving in Torremolinos where, to our consternation, we learned that Gordon, Gwen and Tony had departed. They had returned to Ibiza!

Vicki, who on Ibiza had been Gordon's girlfriend, welcomed us and invited us to share her apartment, which was situated on the sixth floor of a high building with windows on all sides and which we came to call "The House of Many Winds." Vicki was now married to Ralph Cruet, a tall gray-haired gentleman whom we came to like tremendously. While we were there Relph fell down a flight of stairs and got himself a spectacular black eye, and we began calling him Lucky Ralph because he had escaped with his life.

Above Torremolinos lie the hills of Andalusia. These are rolling hills like the downs of southern England, specked with little white villages far away. One day we set off in the VW with the top down—Ralph, Vicki, Norma, John and I—and drove up into the hills to Ronda. We stopped often to pick flowers, so that the car was soon bedecked with them. Whenever we came to a village, Ralph would stand up and throw flowers to the children as we passed. The scenery was utterly beautiful. Eventually we turned south and came out into the town Marbella, where there is a fine yacht harbor and many beautiful houses, most of which are inhabited by English expatriates.

After several weeks we took leave of marvelous Torremolinos. We drove north into France along the Riviera, into Monaco where we booked into a casino but did not spend any money there, then along the *corniche* over the top of Italy and into Trieste, a strange and mysterious town which I wish I'd had more time to explore, and down into Dalmatia.

The Dalmatian coast is pleasant, but not as spectacularly scenic as some of the travel guides would have you think. The ancient city of Dubrovnik, however, is an interesting place, and seems very medieval. From Dubrovnik we left the coast road and drove eastward into the interior of Dalmatia, over some mountains, and after a day or so came to the old town Pec, which consisted of an ancient and dreary monastary, and a large but dilapidated hotel. Nevertheless we checked into the hotel and took lodging for the night. We found that the rooms and especially the bathrooms were even more dilapidated than we might have expected. At dinnertime we went into the dining room, which was pleasant enough, and were handed menus. The menu was of a sort to be found all over eastern Europe; it opened out into two pages and listed hundreds of dishes of many degrees of elegance, but the only ones available were those to which were affixed a price, and these were usually very few. Leaving Pec we drove south into Macedonia, and the next day into Greece. The change was instant. The Greek towns seemed so clean, bright and cheerful. We turned and drove west to the coast and there took a ferry to the island of Corfu.

John's reading matter at this time, aside from his school-books, consisted mainly of the works of Enid Blyton, and also those of Gerald Durrell, whom he found highly entertaining. It so happened that Durrell at one time had lived on Corfu north of town, and so John required that we visit this hallowed site. As I recall, we failed to locate Durrell's house, but no matter;

John by now had become a naturalist and he insisted that we stop to investigate every strange bug or odd plant that we found alongside the road.

Incidentally, my grandson Glen, who of course is John's son is now at about the age that John was at this time, and he is almost the exact replica of John in this naturalistic proclivity. Both were and are handsome kids; both were and are well behaved and highly intelligent, and I am proud of them both. But, I suppose, this is neither here nor there.

Corfu is a beautiful island with unique scenery. Conspicuous are the ancient olive trees, which stand with scraggly, lightning-blasted branches and very little foliage. They don't ever seem to die.

We finally took up residence at Madam Adriana's Taverna, or guest house. Madam Adriana was a short, not quite plump lady about fifty years old, dark-haired, sharp-featured, shrewd, and not at all reluctant to extract a few more dollars than absolutely necessary from the American tourists. However, we got along fairly well with her, mainly because we were willing to run errands for her. She had no car, and often when she wanted something we were obliged to provide transportation. On one particular occasion we took her to market to buy corn-on-the-cob, and therefore we expected to have corn-on-the-cob for dinner. But when dinner came, the corn-on-the-cob failed to materialize.

No matter. We were comfortable. Across the water, we could see the dread land of Albania where, so we were told, if we rode across in a boat and landed on the shores, we would be seized and killed.

As always, Norma and I worked, producing fiction. Every night in the saloon there was Greek music played, very loudly, and dancing, and this Greek music still reverberates in my mind.

One day Harry Barker, an Englishman from Manchester, appeared on the scene. He and his wife Esmé had come to Corfu as part of a tourist group now residing in a nearby hotel. As Norma and I wandered here and there, we naturally encountered a large number of people, and a few linger very sharply in my memory. These naturally include Gordon, Gwen and Tony, Reynolds Packard from Positano, Ralph Cruet from Torremolinos, and to this list I now add Harry Barker, who was a constant source of amusing ploys and enterprises. One day he and I evolved a scheme which we thought might make for a memorable evening. He should enroll five or six of his fellows from the tour group, then we would approach Madam Adriana. She would be asked to procure the carcass of a sheep and arrange it on a spit over the firepit in a field on the other side of the taverna. There Harry and I would light the fire and turn the spit, thus roasting the lamb. Madam Adriana said yes, it was an admirable plan, but her nephew would be in charge of the cooking because he was an expert and knew exactly how to use the spit and how to baste the meat with the proper Greek seasonings.

So it was settled, and so it occurred. The group, with Harry Barker and myself, gathered in the dining area on the terrace, while on the field Adriana's nephew and a gaggle of children including John, turned the lamb over the fire and, presumably, applied the Greek condiments. The lamb was a long time in cooking, but it made no difference; we sat on the terrace drinking wine. Incidentally, this was not the retsina one usually associates with Greek cuisine, but ordinary red wine. In due course, apparently, the lamb was cooked and taken into the kitchen. Madam Adriana brought some bread and olives to the table, and left us to wait. We waited, and waited more. Eventually, Madam Adriana served us some plates containing bones and gristle, which we looked at with raised eyebrows, while in the kitchen Madam Adriana and all her relatives were feasting.

A few days later Harry Barker and Esmé left Corfu, and shortly thereafter so did we. Back on the mainland we drove south into the Peloponnesus and ended up at Pylos, at the southern tip of Greece. From Pylos we drove to Athens, where we spent two or three days. I must admit that I was not enthralled with the city and spent most of the time in our hotel room writing, while Norma and John went to visit the Acropolis.

From Athens we made our way into Turkey, where we discovered the Turkish drivers to be the most volatile and reckless in the world. I have never seen such insanity on the road. We needed to cash some traveler's checks, but could not find any banks open, so we lived on pistachio nuts for two days before we managed to do so.

At Istanbul we did a good deal of walking, visited the Hagia Sophia, and took an excursion up and down the Golden Horn in a boat full of other tourists. After three or four days we departed for Bulgaria.

At the border we expected—since Bulgaria at this time was a communist country—to be subjected to a dozen tedious formalities, searches and interrogations, but to our surprise we drove past the border post with scarcely a nod from a disinterested matron officer, and with no more fuss than if we had entered France or Italy.[14]

Somewhere along the road through Bulgaria, we stopped at a village grocery to buy a loaf of bread. Outside the door was a queue of women, at least twenty of them, waiting to get into the shop. Norma went to stand at the end of the queue, but when the local ladies saw her they insisted, in a humbling display of good-naturedness, that she come to the head of the queue. I do not know why Norma was extended this privilege. Norma, grateful but embarrassed, at first demurred, but the ladies persisted and all but hustled her to the fore. We enjoyed the bread, but it was almost an anti-climax after being so charmed by these Bulgarian village women.

---

14. I should add that the same was true when we drove through Romania and Hungary, both also part of the Eastern Bloc at this time. Nobody took the slightest interest in our activities, and everyone we encountered in these countries was extremely friendly.

One evening we entered an establishment which I can only describe as a hybrid of restaurant and nightclub, where the entertainment was provided by the "Mickey Maus Orchestra." This ensemble consisted of piano, accordion and drums. They were playing a close facsimile of American jazz, so we made their acquaintance and had them sign a beer label, which is now découpaged into the ceiling of our bar among many other beer labels.

The next night we stopped at an ancient monestary, a picturesque building, and slept in what was formerly a monk's cell. In the morning we continued north and passed through Rose Valley, just below the Balkan mountains. The name itself is sufficiently descriptive of this place, but I will say that the perfume of roses pervaded the air of the vicinity for miles around. The region for centuries has exported a famous attar derived from these valley roses. We learned that an inordinate number of blooms were required to produce one ounce of attar. We purchased a small bottle as a keepsake.

Crossing the Danube we entered Romania, drove to Bucharest and spent the night. The next day we drove up the country to the north and visited the famous painted churches of Moldoviṭa. These are fairy-tale structures beautifully decorated in patterns of color, predominantly blue and white. After a day or two we turned south, then west, into the Carpathian Basin and Transylvania.

The Carpathians are dramatically beautiful mountains, reminiscent of the Alps in truncated form, and lacking the snowfields, glaciers and large lakes. At their edge lies Bran Castle, once the seat of Vlad, that Wallachian voivode known as "the Impaler" and possibly the inspiration for Dracula.

I have not delved seriously into the history of the real Vlad, but it appears that he was a very impatient man and did not take kindly to argument. Rather than propound a reasonable response to an affront, he would instead make a signal and the overzealous offender would be taken aside and impaled on a stake. A famous anecdote tells of a visiting envoy from Braşov whom Vlad invited as a guest to a royal banquet. When asked whether he enjoyed the meal, the envoy complained about the stench issuing from the many impaled bodies which made up the skyline. Vlad looked at the envoy sidelong, eyebrows raised, and said: "Then by all means we must find you a higher seat, where you will not find the stench so offensive." And Vlad gave his signal.

Leaving Transylvania we pushed west through Hungary, Austria, and into Germany. We stopped for breath at the lovely Bavarian city Passau, which is situated on the spot where three rivers meet: the Danube, the Inn and the Ilz.

By some means or another we had got wind of a science-fiction gathering soon to convene at Heidelberg. We drove there and presented ourselves at the hall, where we found Poul Anderson, John Campbell, Alan Nourse and a few others we knew. Heidelberg, of course, is the site of one of the oldest universities in Europe, and where there are universities to be found, there are also taverns. We discovered several such wonderful old establishments. In one of these was a lifesize replica of a lion, or perhaps a real taxidermied specimen, mane and all, that roared at half-hour intervals, I suppose to wake people up and remind them to order another stein of beer.

After the convention we were ready to return home. We drove south from Heidelberg into France to Bordeaux, and there bordered the *Michigan*, a cargo-passenger steamship which, after crossing the Atlantic, discharged us and our Volkswagen at Panama.

Gordon, Gwen and Tony, some time before, had visited Bogotá in Colombia, where Gordon had met Carolina, a woman from a socially prominent local family. Gordon and Carolina had married. Gwen and Tony at this time were still in Ibiza, but Gordon remained in Bogotá.

We telephoned Gordon from Panama and he was anxious to see us. He sounded lonely. We boarded a plane and flew to Bogotá. We remained there several weeks, and on one occasion drove south into the jungle where the family owned a coffee-growing *finca*. We spent several days there before returning to Bogotá.

Gordon, I thought, had made a terrible mistake in marrying Carolina. Not that she wasn't a perfectly nice lady; to the contrary, she was. But she refused to leave Colombia, an impossible predicament for so deep-dyed an Englishman as Gordon, who as a consequence was languishing of homesickness. Yet in true English fashion he never complained of this to Carolina.

We returned to Panama, jumped in our Volkswagen and started north along the Pan-American Highway. There were many borders to be crossed on the way north, and at every border the routine was the same. On the south side of the border would be immigration, police and customs. Then once we had passed through, on the north side there would be customs, police and immigration. For each of these individuals a *mordita* was required, so that every time we crossed a border there would be six *morditas* involved. At one border we found one gentleman on duty who had evolved a racket. He asked to see the registration certificate of the Volkswagen, which he checked with the engine number. He found that there had been a mistake; instead of a nine there was a six, or something similar. He looked at me with a sober face and said, "*Señor*, this is a very serious situation. I can hardly believe that you have stolen this vehicle, but the evidence is…interesting."

I wordlessly opened my wallet, gave him $5; he nodded, went back to his hut; we drove through, and that was that.

The trip up through Central America to California was very pleasant indeed. We found that in every town, no matter what size, there was always a Chinese restaurant, and this was where we generally took our meals. At one town in Mexico, we came upon an ice cream parlor which advertised 57 flavors, including avocado. Yet when we looked into the place and inquired after some of the more exotic varieties of ice cream, we discovered that only two were presently available: chocolate and vanilla.

We drove up through Nogales into Arizona, then into California, and so after many a weary mile once again arrived home, where as usual we kissed the ground and joyfully resumed our old routines.

Pale hands I loved beside the Shalimar,
Where are you now? Who lies beneath your spell?
—LAURENCE HOPE

CHAPTER 9

IN 1974, WHEN John was thirteen years old, we found ourselves in funds again and set off once more to travel around the world. Parenthetically, there ought to be a word to describe this sort of travel; circumnavigation is when you travel the world by sea, but to the best of my knowledge there is no corresponding word to specify traveling around the world by land or air.

We flew from Oakland to Shannon Airport, where we rented a car and set off across the Irish countryside. We went first to Cong, in County Mayo, then drove another seven miles along the north shore of Loch Coirib, and visited our former landlords the Molloys. On this occasion we undertook a venture which we previously had neglected. Behind our old cottage rose Mt. Gable. We climbed to the summit and were rewarded by a view of awe-inspiring magnificence. To the south spread Loch Coirib, all the way to Galway. To the north we overlooked the even larger expanse of Loch Maske.

We also encountered a mystery which to this day remains unsolved. This was a rick containing two or three hundred peat slabs.[15] Yet since there was no road leading up to the summit of Mt. Gable, and certainly no peat bogs for miles around, the circumstances were more than puzzling.

In due course we took our leave of the Molloys and drove eastward through County Mayo to County Meath, where we visited the town Kells and the abbey where, in 800 A.D., Celtic monks had produced what is now known as Ireland's most precious national treasure: *The Book of Kells*. At Trinity College we visited the glass-topped case which allows passersby to view one page of this marvelously illuminated manuscript. Every day a steward opens the case and turns the page, so that if some diligent bibliophile wished to make a daily pilgrimage to this quadrangle for a year or so, he might view the entire book.

Leaving County Meath we returned to Shannon, where we turned in our car, boarded a plane and flew to Paris. There we rented another car and proceeded south through the wonderful French countryside, into Spain, and eventually arrived at Torremolinos, where we sought out our friends Ralph and Vicky Cruet, whom we had known before on Ibiza. They put us up in their apartment on the top floor of a tower which we called "The House of Many Winds." After a week or so we drove westward into Portugal and ultimately to Lisbon, where we turned in our car and boarded another plane, this bound for Madeira.

Madeira, as is well known, is a beautiful island and at this time was a favorite resort of British holiday-makers. We rented an apartment about a mile outside Funchal, where we remained for about a month. Needless to say, I occupied myself with writing, and occasionally taking tea at Reed's Hotel, which during the days of the British Empire had ranked with the best in the world.

---

15. If anyone is interested, peat is extracted from bogs using a spadelike instrument known as a *slane*. It is thrown up on the bank and allowed to dry and mature for several months; the end product is used all over Ireland as a fuel. When we were in residence at the Molloy cottage we used it in our fireplace. It burns beautifully, makes a lovely fire and produces a sharp, woodsy odor, which once smelled is never forgotten, and which for me is indelibly linked to memories of Ireland.

When our sojourn on Madeira came to an end, we boarded the steamer *Reina del Mar* and set sail across the south Atlantic toward Capetown, South Africa.

Our passage on this vessel was a dream voyage. John made friends with six or seven other children of his own age, English émigrés to South Africa. When we landed at Capetown John was heartbroken to be separated from his new friends. Once ashore, we bought a white Volkswagen Beetle distinguished by a big yellow butterfly painted on its rear end. We also bought a tent and camping gear, and drove south to a campground at Fish Hoek. To say that this first camp was not a success is an understatement. It was almost a disaster. We had a terrible time getting the tent up; it had wooden stakes which broke, and the wind blew and flapped the fabric of the tent almost out of control. Moreover the campsite itself was unpleasant. Norma and John took a gondola up to the top of Table Mountain, but John was still disconsolate with the loss of his friends and did not much enjoy himself.

The next day we struck camp and drove east to another campground at George. This site was far more pleasant than Fish Hoek. We remained there a week, made a few acquaintances and perfected our camping skills before moving on to other pleasant campgrounds, among these one near Graaff Reinet, a picturesque town distinguished by quaint old Dutch architecture.

We pitched our tent under a tree and set up "housekeeping;" I wrote, and for recreation played my banjo ukelele. One morning we noticed that a baby bird, probably a sparrow, had fallen from its nest and lay on the ground. John took the bird into the tent and fed it milk, bread crumbs, bits of seed, and anything he felt would restore its health; in due course it convalesced and became a pet. John named the bird Dagwood. Dagwood eventually learned to fly, first around the tent, then outside, where we wished to see if he would fly away. Dagwood flew up into a tree, but whenever we had our breakfast or lunch, he would fly down, perch himself on the plate, and help himself to whatever suited his appetite. Dagwood had evidently identified us as his parents.

One morning as I sat outside the tent playing my banjo uke, a gentleman approached and introduced himself as Bob Kok. He lived in Krugersdorp, a town near Durban on South Africa's west coast, and identified himself as a jazz enthusiast. Upon hearing me play my ukelele, he felt compelled to approach us and pass the time of day. He said that he had once been instrumental in bringing Lionel Hampton and his band from the United States to Durban. Later, when we were in Durban we visited Bob in his home, we met his wife Leone and their four beautiful daughters. They lived in a most pleasant house, with a swimming pool and a fine garden.[16]

Departing the pleasant campground at Graaff Reinet, and reluctantly leaving Dagwood to carry on as best he could, we drove north through a game preserve, where we saw a rhinoceros and an elephant but no lions, then continued into Rhodesia, where we did not immediately camp but went to the city of Salisbury and took up residence in the hotel there.

John needed a haircut, so I took him to one of the town barbers. Before we entered the shop, Johnny halted me and instructed me to watch the barber very carefully, to make sure that he did not cut off too much hair and "make his ears stick out like seashells." I assured him of my vigilance and he took his place in the barber's chair. I seated myself where I could watch, but my attention became diverted by a magazine, possibly *Playboy* or something similar, and I forgot to guard John from the barber's zeal. When I looked up, John had already received a good roaching, so that only a tuft stuck out on the top

---

16. Years later, there was a knock on our door in Oakland, and who should appear but Bob Kok. He had a sad story to tell. His daughters had all married and had left home, his wife had died, and Bob Kok was now a very lonesome man. He stayed with us for a while, then returned to South Africa. This was the last we ever heard of him.

of his head. When the barber whisked off the cloth, John looked in the mirror and discovered that his fears had been realized. He turned me a look of death, glaring but saying nothing. I felt guilty as hell, but it wasn't long before his hair grew out again.

While in Rhodesia we visited the Great Zimbabwe National Monument, an ancient city of mystery. Nobody is sure who built these spectacular ruins, but the latest theory holds that they are the work of native Africans. Rhodesia is now known as Zimbabwe; evidently the native people had no wish immortalize the name of Sir Cecil Rhodes.

We continued north to Victoria Falls and pitched our tent on the adjacent campground. A trail led from the campground through the jungle to the falls, which were indeed stupendous. Watching them, we were soaked in spray and fog, but the spectacle was well worth a bit of moisture.

Back at the campground, I entered a little shop where I found ebony logs for sale. These logs were perhaps a foot long, and four or five inches in diameter. The exterior was still sheathed in bark, and they showed a ring of white wood surrounding a core of black beautiful ebony. In the United States, of course, ebony is extremely expensive. Here at Victoria Falls, the price was something around a dollar apiece. I bought two logs, packed them into our suitcases and eventually brought them home.

From Victoria Falls we drove south, through Durban to a beautiful campground at a place called Port St. John, on the coast. We settled down beside a little stream, and set to work, producing my regulation two or three thousand words a day, instructing John in his long-distance schooling. Norma went about her duties as well.

After a time, we left Port St. John and drove north to Durban, where we took up residence in the inexpensive but surprisingly pleasant Lucy's Hotel. At the American Express office, we learned of the *Karanja*, a ship which shortly would be putting in to Durban, then proceeding on to Karachi, with stops en route at Beira, Dar es Salaam and Mombasa. The fare was most reasonable, so we booked passage.

The *Karanja* turned out to be an old rustbucket, not at all handsome, yet still capable of making a coastwise trip, and so in due course we went aboard and sailed out of Durban. Aboard the ship drinks were 10¢ a shot. The cuisine was fair-to-middling, in general quite decent. They had two menus: one Indian, and the other Anglo-Saxon.

We put in to Beira and saw the sights, then continued north to Mombasa, where the *Karanja* remained three or four days; during this interval Norma and I took occasion to visit a game park under Mt. Kilimanjaro. We rented a car to drive there, and found a beautiful hotel beside the water hole. During our stay we saw elephants, zebras and antelope, but no lions or anything alarming.

We left the *Karanja* at Karachi, which, we decided, lacked charm. My most vivid recollection is the *muezzin's* call at sunrise—one of the most mournful, lonesome sounds imaginable.

From Karachi we traveled north by train. Halfway to Rawalpindi we left the train and, braving ferocious heat, explored the ruins of Mohenjo-daro, an ancient civilization coeval with Babylon, inhabited by a mysterious people about whom not much is known.

At Rawalpindi we took up residence in Flashman's Hotel, an old English establishment straight out of Kipling. Then we continued east into India, where we boarded an airplane and flew north to Srinagar in the Kashmir Valley beside Dal Lake, known for its hundreds of houseboats originally built for British officials during the days of the *Raj*. Despite the houseboats, Dal Lake was not a particular inspiring vista, so we went on to Nagin Lake, which was another story: smaller but more beautiful, surrounded by trees and mountains. There were fewer houseboats here, but these were much more attractive than those on Lake

Dal. We found the houseboat "Bluebird" to our taste and rented it, settling down for a period of work.

The owner of the houseboat, Mr. Khan-Kashi, lived ashore and cooked our meals on an outdoor grill over a firepit. We spent three idyllic months at Lake Nagin, both Norma and I working hard. I sat at a chair in the window looking out across the water, while Norma kept a small desk nearby. Every day long flat-bottomed boats would ply the lake, each sculled by a pair of men who worked to harvest water-weeds which they used to fertilize their crop plots and gardens. They loaded the boats until they almost submerged, with the gunwales underwater! Only constant bailing kept the boats from sinking. Daily as I sat in my window, peddlers would drift by, selling fruits and vegetables, flowers and a few items of general miscellany.

Two flower-vendors visited us at regular intervals. They were Mr. Marvelous and Mr. Wonderful. Mr. Marvelous would come aboard the houseboat, throw out everything Mr. Wonderful had left for us and replace it with flowers of his own. The next day Mr. Wonderful would arrive and do the same, vice-versa. Norma and I found their activities amusing, and didn't interfere with them—especially because their prices were so moderate.

In Srinagar we bought three rugs and arranged to have them shipped home to Oakland. We also ventured into a woodworker's shop owned by a Mr. Peer, with whom we struck up what would become a very pleasant association. I ordered a hundred or so urn-shaped objects which I intended to put around our buffet at home as a kind of rail; this idea was later realized and turned out as beautifully as I had envisioned. I also made arrangements with Mr. Peer for some further woodwork which I would order by mail as soon as I got home. When we made our departure, Mr. Peer saw us off at the airport, and he wept to see us go. He was truly a charming gentleman.

Upon leaving Kashmir we made our way south to Jaipur to see the Taj Mahal, which we viewed at midnight as well as by day. From Jaipur we went further south to Udaipur, where we stayed the night in a palace converted into a hotel on an island in the middle of the lake, a famous tourist attraction. From Udaipur we proceeded to Bombay for a few days, then further south to Kerala. We put up in a splendid hotel and dined at a table which was about fifty yards distant from the hotel itself, so that the waiters had to cross an expanse of lawn in order to serve us. However, they made no complaints about this peculiar distance.

We made a number of expeditions into the surrounding countryside. We saw pepper trees and a teak plantation. Teak trees are planted very densely, only about three feet apart, so that they grow straight up without any branches. This way they achieve great heights and yield teak timber of straight grain and devoid of knots and other imperfections.

During our stay in Kerala, we failed to visit two of the most impressive and romantic locales in India. The first of these is a jungle interlaced by canals; tourists can hire a boat which is sculled through these canals by a boatman. It is said that these canals are overhung by orchids and other beautiful flowers and that this is a wonderful experience. The second is one of the hill-stations, which during the days of the Raj, the British would visit to avoid the heat of summer. There are two principal hill-stations: one is Simla in the north, and in the south, in Tamil Nadu there is Ootacamund. Access to Ootacamund is either by road or air, and also by railroad. The train route is said to be extremely beautiful.

To my endless regret we neglected to visit Ootacamund and instead flew south to Sri Lanka, then known as Ceylon. There we lodged ourselves in Colombo, the capital, at the Galle Face, a grand old colonial hotel overlooking the ocean. Arthur C. Clarke was a resident of Colombo, and I took occasion to call on him. We had lunch at his house, and he showed us the film *2001: A Space Odyssey*. He enjoyed building complicated structures using erector set components. He built bridges, buildings, machinery, and anything else his fertile imagination might conceive. Clarke was also interested in diving, and he gave John a book he had written containing information as to the best places to dive in Ceylon, including a coral reef across the island, where we later did some snorkeling.

After a week in Colombo we moved down the coast to a resort called Hikkaduwa, where we lodged ourselves in a hotel which happened not only to be very pleasant but also astonishingly inexpensive. John, exploring the reef, saw a lionfish in a pool and was much impressed. Norma and I worked. However, our stay was truncated because our visas stipulated a visit of only one month.

We next flew east to Singapore, where naturally, like homing pigeons, we went to the Raffles hotel. To maximize the romance, we went directly to the bar, where Norma and I put down Singapore Slings. Johnny had an orange soda. After a day or so we changed our lodgings to a much less expensive Chinese hotel, which was austere but extremely clean and well managed. In town, I found that musical instruments were astonishingly inexpensive, so I bought two banjos, one long-neck, one short-neck, for $40 apiece. One of the squares in town served a double purpose: by day it functioned as a market, while at night foodsellers gathered, and by the light of lanterns and candles served all manner of delicacies, among the most memorable of which was *satay*.

After about a week in Singapore we flew to Sumatra, where we visited a batik factory, then to Java, where we visited that ninth-century Buddhist monument known as the Borobudur, beside which stands an enormous and ancient banyan tree. From Java we went on to the enchanted island of Bali.

The tourist brochures describe Bali in perhaps rhapsodic terms, but this cannot be anything but understatement. Bali is indescribable. I won't try to disprove that statement, because I would just go on for pages and pages. I will only mention one afternoon when we sat drinking some Balinesian concoction of passionfruit juice and gin, and listening to the gamelan music. This is an ancient music of mysterious origin, strange to western ears and sensibilities. Eight or ten musicians sit with gongs, bells and instruments of the sort, making a sound that ripples like water. To western ears this music has no form; no melody can be made out—and yet, the musicians know precisely what they are doing. They all stop at the same instant, seemingly without cue. I found gamelan music intensely beautiful, even though I did not understand it.

Among the other wonderful aspects of Bali are the Balinese themselves. We found them to be utterly kind, pleasant people, again worthy of any superlatives I might be inclined to use.

Leaving Bali we flew back to Singapore, and then to Borneo, and here we embarked on what I can only call an adventure. A young lady, acting as our guide, took us to a river where we boarded a dugout about twenty-five feet long, powered by an outboard motor, and set us off up the river. We went through jungle, saw monkeys swinging through the trees, and finally— after six or seven hours!—arrived at a Dayak longhouse.

Dayaks are the native inhabitants of Borneo, and in those times were still considered somewhat savage. Leaving the boat, we climbed into the longhouse, where our guide spoke at length with the chief, apparently making arrangements. The longhouse was a single room lacking all furnishing, floored with matting. We were instructed to sit on this. As we did so we noticed a number of shrunken heads hanging from the rafters. The guide noticed our apprehension and reassured us that we had nothing to fear; these were the heads of Japanese captured during the war. We were shown to particular mats on the floor upon which we would sleep, covered by mosquito netting. Here we sat, watching these presumably savage Dayaks going about their daily business, the children laughing and joking, the women talking together about heaven knows what.

An hour or two passed while we sat marveling at this remarkable adventure in the wild interior of Borneo. We heard a noise outside, and up the steps into the longhouse came a girl leading a party of five or six German tourists, all chattering at once. Our bubble of wonder was rudely broken.

The next day we returned downriver and flew back to Singapore, then to Hong Kong, and finally back to Oakland.

I love this little house because
It offers, after dark,
A pause for rest, a rest for paws,
A place to moor my bark.
—ARTHUR GUITERMAN, *MOTTO FOR A DOGHOUSE*

CHAPTER 10

ONE SUMMER, AFTER we had been home for a while, we thought that John might enjoy visiting the Molloys in Ireland by himself for a period. John was a little dubious, but nevertheless we communicated with Mary Molloy, who said she would be glad to have him, and we put John on an airplane. He spent a month in Ireland, during which time we had some letters from him which were rather woebegone and sad; he was not having a good time. So we arranged to fly him back, and there down the runway came John with an expression on his face which was indescribable. Of course we were delighted to see him. We took him to Spenger's Fish Grotto, which was at that time a great restaurant, where John ordered his favorite dish, shrimp scatter. Then we went home, and learned that John had been homesick and lonesome, and that the whole episode had been a very grim failure. Of course Norma and I felt like dogs.

During this period of my life I was often invited to science fiction conventions. Every year there would be one important grand convention and a number of lesser ones. For the most part I was disinclined to participate in these conventions, except when I was invited as guest of honor and therefore could not decline gracefully. My duties were to sign books, to be polite to people, and sometimes to give a speech.

At first I prepared my speeches and memorized them, only to find at the podium that I had forgotten the speech and was forced to improvise. In due course I discovered a method to avoid this embarrassment. It is the simplest, easiest way to address an audience. To wit: the speaker prepares no speech whatever. He announces that he has prepared no speech but will take questions from the audience. Anyone who wishes to ask questions may raise his hand and the speaker will answer. This tactic, so I have found, seems to satisfy everybody.

I have attended conventions in Los Angeles, Palm Beach, Seattle, Medicine Hat (Alberta, Canada), and Melbourne, Australia, as well as in the Netherlands, Sweden, France and Germany.

John and I attended the convention in Melbourne together. There we were joined by the writer Terry Dowling, a charming young man who played the guitar and sang comic songs on Australian television and who was great fun to be with, and who to this day remains one of our closest friends.

After the convention in Melbourne, Johnny and I drove to Sydney. On the way we spent the night in the Hydro Majestic Hotel, a palatial edifice situated on a cliff in the Blue Mountains overlooking the Megalong Valley. At this time the hotel was in a state of sad disrepair, with hardly a working toilet in the establishment. For the evening's entertainment, a young lady played unaccompanied clarinet very badly. We learned that the world-famous Graeme Bell had been there playing piano the night before. Bell led a great Australian jazz band, in which he also played piano; his brother Roger Bell played cornet; a chap named "Lazy Ade" Monsborough played trombone.

Terry tells me that since the time of our visit, the Hydro Majestic Hotel was been renovated and is now a beautiful luxury establishment.

More recently, while Norma and I were attending a convention in Tours, France, our friend Paul Rhoads took us on a memorable excursion through the French countryside. He had heard that the best cassoulet in France was to be found at a certain restaurant in the south. We decided to test this rumor. We drove south and ultimately found this restaurant. It was off in the country, down a side road, and occupied a rather barnlike structure. We went in, prepared ourselves to sample the best cassoulet in the world. We ordered it and then waited for what must have been an hour before it arrived at our table. And… it was just terrible. In fact, it was almost inedible. So much for that!

While I am on the subject of French cuisine, I am impelled to recall an episode which occurred long ago while we were touring France, when John was only about eight years old. I mentioned that we traveled by the Michelin guide, following the red rocking chairs, and also by the designations of the restaurants. The three-star restaurants, of course, are the best. There was a certain restaurant that had received a three-star rating for many years, and everyone seemed to concede that it was probably the best restaurant in France. This was La Pyramide. One Sunday, we chanced to be in the neighborhood,[17] and decided to stop in at La Pyramide for lunch, despite the fact that we were dressed very casually and might even have been described as scruffy Americans. Nevertheless, we were met at the door by Madame Point. Monsieur Point, who originated La Pyramide, had died, leaving the restaurant in the capable hands of his wife. She greeted us most graciously, seated us, and there we enjoyed one of the most magnificent meals of our lives. I am reasonably certain that Norma agreed with this assessment. John, I regret to say, had chosen to remain in the car reading Gerald Durrell, and so missed out on this gastronomic *tour de force*. Norma and I

---

17. Vienne.

subsequently tried several other three-star restaurants in France, but none of them came up to the standard of La Pyramide.[18]

On the occasion of the science fiction convention in Stockholm, I went alone. I flew via Icelandic Airways to England, then ferried from Newcastle upon Tyne in Yorkshire to Bergen, Norway. There I rented a car and drove through the Norwegian countryside. This is beyond question the most beautiful scenery I have ever seen anywhere, what with fjords and mountains, forests and fields. The time was summer, so the sun set late and rose early, and there didn't seem to be any night at all.

During my drive through Norway occurred one of the most terrifying experiences of my life. Along the road through the countryside I came to a tunnel. As I started through I reached down to turn on my headlights, only to find that I did not know where the headlight controls were! I was already well in the tunnel and could hardly back up, and I saw a luminous patch perhaps a tenth of a mile ahead, which marked the exit from the tunnel. This was the longest tenth of a mile I have ever traversed in my life. It never occurred to me that I might have blown my horn to alert other drivers. Instead I crossed my fingers on the steering wheel and aimed the car for the little spot of light at the far end of the tunnel. By some miracle I never brushed the walls of the tunnel, and by another miracle I emerged from it un-scathed. When I got out I stopped the car by the side of the road to let my rattled nerves settle down. Although I didn't jump out and kiss the ground, I certainly felt like it.

The rental car was expensive, and I only drove it for four or five days before taking public transportation to Stockholm. The convention, which was sponsored by a Swedish aristocrat, went about as usual: I was asked to give a speech, but on this occasion

18. I am sad to report that La Pyramide no longer exists; Mme. Point and her culinary delights are now things of the past. I am told the restaurant died with her; and perhaps this is a more romantic fate than the long, slow decline typical of so many establishments after their originators have departed.

it took place in the dining room instead of on a stage with a podium. It therefore was not convenient to invite people to ask questions, as they were busy dining and drinking, so I talked, gave my opinions, produced wise remarks. As I talked I noticed a faint buzz; I went on, but noticed the buzz growing louder and louder. Somewhere, in the middle of a sentence, I stopped talking, sat down, and nobody seemed to notice.

On my return home I stopped in Copenhagen, Denmark for a day or two. After checking into a hotel I went to explore the city. On a certain street where pedestrians only are allowed—no wheeled traffic—I sat on a bench to enjoy the sunshine and watch the passersby. Presently a lady came down and sat beside me. She was about forty years old, and not particularly handsome or well dressed. She began talking, telling me about herself. It seemed she worked in a saloon. Before long, she not-too-subtly propositioned me, and it dawned on me that this lady was on the make. I politely declined her proposition and moved on. Halfway toward the hotel, I noticed a young lady leaning against a car parked at the curb. She called out to me, and I thought to hear her use my name. I stopped and turned an inquiring gaze on her. Then this woman, too, propositioned me. She was younger and considerably more attractive than the lady of my previous encounter, but still—no sale. A hundred yards further along, an even younger woman—a girl, in fact, no more than fifteen or sixteen years old, skinny, with wild dark hair—darted out and extended me the third proposition of the day. I made haste back to my hotel, where I vowed to stay clear of that particular street on my next visit to Copenhagen.

Back in Oakland it was life as usual again. We continued to work on our house, which was now almost complete. In the place of the original, dilapidated little shack was now a three-story structure which I will not quite call a mansion, but which was spacious and comfortable. Before we could finish our dining room it was necessary to dig out some more of the hillside and put in a retaining wall. This we did, and built a beautiful stone wall using the stones which Norma and I over the years had brought up from the Mojave desert. At the opposite end of the room we installed a bar surfaced in polished mahogany and surrounded by horse brasses we had collected in England. Gradually we stocked the bar, not all at once but whenever we could afford the investment, so that over time it acquired many bottles of various distillations and tinctures and extracts.

My grandfather, in the library of his home on Haight Street in San Francisco, had owned a collection of *Life* magazines, archived by year in great leather-bound volumes from 1883 to 1936. Here, it must be noted, I am referring not to Henry Luce's later pictorial magazine of the same name, but to the original old humor magazine inspired by *Puck*, which in turn was the American answer to the British magazine *Punch*. When I was young and stayed with my grandfather, every night I would take to bed several volumes of *Life* and look them over until I fell asleep. About thirty years ago I came upon such a leather-bound collection for sale. This collection, however, was truncated at about 1917. The price was right, however, so I bought the collection, and it remains today on our bookshelves. These are wonderful magazines, and after about 1900 equal to *Punch*. They contain many full-page illustrations by Harrison Cady, who later went on to illustrate the Thornton Burgess books regarding Reddy the Fox and Chatterer the Red Squirrel, et al. Gibson is present and shows us his eponymous girls. The automobiles of the day were advertised in every spare inch, as was, depicted in the most romantically illustrated panels, a product called Creme Yvette, a liquor flavored with violet and vanilla which, sadly, is no longer manufactured. The artist behind these advertisements must be commended, as his work performed its function so successfully that years later, when the opportunity offered to augment the facilities of my bar with Creme Yvette, I seized upon it.

I hope that this discussion regarding my bar and its multiple contents will not create the perception that I am an alcoholic. This is far from the truth. I admit that I regard the evening cocktail hour as a noble institution, but not an indispensable one. We often had wine with our dinner.

Last year, my friend Jeremy Cavaterra and I chanced upon some old Trader Vic's recipes, specifically the original Mai Tai and the Scorpion, and we became so vitalized by these that we began to formulate a unique and extraordinary series of libations which are to be found nowhere else but in this particular corner of Oakland. These include the "Stuttercup," "Valley View Up-and-Down," "Coyote Varnish," as well as a few realizations of hypothetical concoctions from my books, such as "Blue Ruin" and "Pooncho Punch." Again, I assert that while I am by no means a wowser, neither could I be called a tapdancing drunk. Still, back in those days of yore, not an evening went by before Jeremy and I looked at each other and asked if the sun had gone down over the yardarm yet.[19]

Once a month or so Norma and I visited the town of Three Rivers in the Sierra Nevada foothills south of Yosemite. Here every Friday night, the High Sierra Jazz Band played. The band was made up of all local musicians, and was absolutely superb. I don't remember the names of all the personnel apart from Al Smith, who played trumpet.

On one of Terry Dowling's visits, we took him to Three Rivers. About halfway there we stopped in Merced for dinner. I had contrived a method by which a transient might locate the best restaurant in town. He must find the local bookshop and take advice from the proprietor, who infallibly will possess this information. Why the bookshop? Because bookshop owners are usually discriminating gourmets without too much money.

---

19. I say "went" because, as I write this, circumstances have changed. Due to certain medical contingencies too dreary to enumerate, I no longer indulge in alcohol, and our bar, except for when family or drinking guests come to stay, is now a quiet place.

In Merced, the bookshop proprietor and his wife recommended a Basque restaurant at the edge of town and mentioned that they themselves would be going there this evening. They invited us to join them, and we were happy to do so. The restaurant proved to be beyond reproach, once again validating my theory.

A Basque restaurant is quite different from the ordinary. You sit at a long table along with many other people, and the cuisine is served family-style. Everything appears on the table at once, from soup onwards. During the meal we became better acquainted with our friends from the bookshop. The proprietor's wife informed us, with as much nonchalance as if she talked about the weather, that they lived in a haunted house.

I raised my eyebrows. "Haunted house? Really?"

"Oh, there's no question about it," the lady declared, "I've seen the ghosts myself."

Terry asked what the ghosts looked like, and the lady went on to describe what she had seen. She was specific in her descriptions; often, for instance, she found the ghosts sitting on her bed, staring at her. I looked to the husband for confirmation; he looked up toward the ceiling, shrugged, but neither endorsed nor contradicted these testimonials.

She further informed us that she had called in a priest to exorcise the house. The priest performed the appropriate rites, sprinkled holy water here and there, and for a time the ghosts were abashed and failed to appear; but before long they returned, and our friends resigned themselves to cohabit with this infestation.

Terry and I expressed an inclination to visit this house, but Norma considered this proposal to be bad form and quietly discouraged us. And so after leaving the excellent Basque restaurant we parted company. The next morning, as we were leaving Merced, we drove past the residence in question, but saw only an ordinary modern suburban house.

The ceiling in our dining room was ordered from our friend, Mr. Peer in Kashmir. I took careful measurements and mailed them off. In due course the shipment arrived, exactly as ordered: pieces of Kashmir walnut, beautifully carved and polished. John did an excellent job installing the wood in the ceiling. With the stone wall and fireplace at one end, and the bar gleaming with horse-brasses at the other, the whole illuminated by the Waterford crystal chandelier, the dining room is now our favorite room in the house.

We continued to improve the house. I had originally installed a slate floor in the living room, which was a tremendous amount of work, something like a jigsaw puzzle since every piece of slate had to be fitted exactly. Eventually we grew dissatisfied with it; the slate had turned a dark, dull purplish green and gave the living room a rather gloomy atmosphere; so we pulled it up and replaced it with a hardwood floor.

The old house is now just about finished, but we often discuss further additions. Building our home has been one of our great pleasures.

Whither, O splendid ship, thy white sails crowding,
Leaning across the bosom of the urgent West?
—ROBERT BRIDGES

CHAPTER 11

BOATS, IN ONE capacity or another, have always been a part of my life. When I was about ten years old, living up at Green Lodge Ranch, I built a boat out of fence rails, canvas and waterproof paint. It was about twelve feet long and sloop-rigged. I carried it over to the sloughs; it floated, did not leak, but neither did it sail worth a darn. Such was my first boat.

I acquired my second boat while working at the Olympic Club. This was a 14-foot sloop which I bought from a bellhop for $40. I don't remember what happened to it; I suppose I sold it. My third boat was also a 14-foot sloop, which I bought while a sophomore at the university. I kept it docked at the Berkeley marina and sailed it here and there around San Francisco Bay.

On one occasion I took John West and Anne Pickering from the *Daily Cal* out sailing. We headed out toward Tiburon, a town in Marin County, but halfway there encountered strong winds and decided to turn back. Then occurred one of the most harrowing experiences of my life. A big wave came up behind us, threw the stern of the boat over. The wind caught the sails the wrong way and knocked us over, and to use a seagoing term, we broached, and all three of us were thrown into the water.

After a moment or two of shock, I tried to right the boat, without a glimmer of success. The shore was two or three miles off, and we could not swim so far, and all of us realized that submersion in this cold water would not do our health any good; in fact we would die of exposure in short order. Fortunately, someone had seen us go over and had notified the coast guard, which presently sent out a rescue boat. They pulled us from the water, but either would not or could not save the boat; it drifted into the Berkeley Pier and broke up among the pilings, which was all very well as I was not too pleased with the conduct of this boat.

Of course, I can make no pretense but to admit that this sorry episode was due to my own bad seamanship. Ever thereafter, even while sailing much larger boats, I retained an obsessional dread of that insidious stroke of destiny known as "the broach."

My friend Tom Hand co-owned this boat, and when we bought it, it was submerged in ten feet of water at Bay Point, a town about fifteen miles up the San Joaquin River. Since Tom Hand was glib and declared an aversion to getting himself wet, I was required to do the diving, down ten feet into the hold, where I found the ballast and carried it to the surface. In due course the boat followed and we set sail back to Berkeley. As we sailed we noticed that the boat leaked, and were forced to bail it out at intervals. So we sailed down the river, under the Carquinez Bridge and out onto San Francisco Bay. Here, among the waves and strong winds, we got very seriously worked, and I went down to bail using a bucket, which I then cast to Tom who would throw the water overboard. But on one of these passes Tom threw the bucket overboard along with the water— a reflex action of some sort—and there was nothing left to bail with. The water was coming in, not exactly in a torrent, but fast enough so that the boat was in serious trouble. I looked around for something to bail with but could find nothing but a bottle. I picked up the bottle and with great care knocked off its neck, and used what remained to scoop up water and threw it out a porthole. Otherwise, the boat would have sunk, Tom Hand and I would have been thrown into the water despite Tom's aversion to being wet, and we would not have returned to the land of the living, since the coast guard was nowhere in evidence. However, through the agency of this broken bottle, the boat remained afloat and ultimately we docked in the Berkeley Marina, where we alighted and kissed the ground. Subsequently we sold the boat to my brother Louis.

The years passed, years quite devoid of boats, although I subscribed to yachting magazines and studied yacht designs with great concentration. Along about this time a description of the Tahiti ketch appeared in *Mechanics Illustrated*. This was truly a romantic boat. A double-ender, about thirty feet long, it was solid, strong, deep-keeled, two-masted: not fast but dependable. The designer claimed that it could sail anywhere back and forth, laugh at storms, and that its design had been derived from the old Viking longboats. I also yearned for a boat of the type called the Block Island ketch. Block Island is off the coast of Rhode Island, and these ketches are used to carry supplies back and forth despite all extremities of weather. They were usually about thirty feet long; the hull showed no concave lines, with an extraordinarily wide beam. The ballast was internal and usually consisted of stone; the masts were unstayed and, at that early time, made of pine trunks (nowadays they are made of carbon fiber).

Eventually, however, my attention was diverted from the Tahiti ketch to the trimaran. This type of boat, for people not in the know, consists of three hulls: a large center hull, then a smaller hull to either side attached with struts. Although the trimaran concept is originally Polynesian and thousands of years old, the model in use today was popularized by Arthur Piver, an American boatbuilder working on the west coast. Piver came to be known as "the father of the modern trimaran." He claimed that the trimaran could sail anywhere in the world without problems. Thousands of adventurous young men and women began to build trimarans using Piver's plans. In 1967 Piver, in order to satisfy requirements to qualify for the forthcoming Observer Singlehanded Trans-Atlantic Race, embarked on a 500-mile solo voyage from San Francisco to San Diego. He never reached port, and has never been seen again.

I've heard it said that on the beaches of Samoa there are hundreds of derelict trimarans which people had sailed from all parts of the world and then abandoned, for one reason or another.

I bought the plans for a 32' Piver trimaran, and built a beautiful main hull before deciding that the vessel was too small for what I considered oceangoing needs. Piver himself had disappeared in a 25-footer. I found a buyer—none other than one of Piver's own assistants—who agreed to pay $1,500 for my half-finished trimaran. He gave me a down-payment of $100 to haul the hull away and then, like Piver himself, vanished without a trace. I saw nothing more of him, or the balance.

For many years the Vance family went boatless, until John's sixteenth birthday when I presented him with a Venture 17' sloop. This was a strong, sturdy, safe little craft which would never think of acting like my wretched boats of yore. John sailed her with enthusiasm back and forth around the bay.

A year or so passed; then during a prosperous phase of our lives we turned the Venture in on a 10.7-meter Columbia sloop. The Columbia was a lovely boat, although John and I both felt that the rigging was rather slight, and we made plans to bolster it, although we never got around to this project. A year or two later, as I was looking through my yachting magazines, I chanced to come upon a design by Stan Huntingford of Vancouver, a 45' ketch—strong, seaworthy and utterly beautiful. I fell in love. By coincidence I learned that an agency at the Alameda marina was selling this particular ketch and already had three in stock on the premises. The progression of events was inevitable. We christened the boat *Hinano*, after the beautiful flowering shrub, and the girl we had known on Tahiti—and the most popular Tahitian brand of beer, a great deal of which we had consumed.

John and I worked on the *Hinano*, beefed her up, improved the rigging, and reinforced it wherever the need seemed to exist, until *Hinano* was a sturdy boat indeed, and we thought we could sail her to the south Pacific without trepidation. Of course Norma would not accompany John and me on this voyage, which we planned to undertake as soon as we had enough money to finance it.

John got more use out of *Hinano* than I did, sailing it all over the bay and along the coast, up to Oregon and back down the coast. John learned celestial navigation; we bought what must have been a hundred charts. These charts are a joy to look at and ponder over, because each will show perhaps some little island, its lagoon and the paths into the lagoon, with all the depths, and if there's a village on the island will indicate this— sheer romance!

I wish I could say that our plans for *Hinano* had matured and that we had put off to sea, sailing out the Golden Gate and heading southwest, but the truth of the matter lies in that oft-quoted apothegm that a boat is defined as a hole in the ocean which you fill with money. What with payments on the boat, upkeep, mooring fees and other expenses, we found that we simply could not rake up enough money to take off and, with great reluctance, we sold *Hinano*.

My brother David has five sons. The oldest is Stephen, then Dana, followed by Kevin, Dwight and Scott. Kevin is in the construction business; Dana is an electrical engineer and lives in Seattle; Dwight is a computer expert; Scott is an actor in Hollywood.

I like all my nephews but I am closest to Steve. All Steve's life we have shared a passion for sailboats. We never tire of talking about their design and construction. Steve has done far more boating than I have. He and his wife Marja sailed around the world in a 27' sloop. They have been so many places that, arriving at any strange port, they are bound to run into acquaintances.

Steve and Marja now work for a private yachtsman: Steve captains the 100' boat and Marja is first mate and cook. They phone me regularly, always from a different part of the world. They are planning to retire soon, but will probably continue to sail in one fashion or another, perhaps touring Europe in a canal boat.

A final word in regard to *Hinano*. She is still, so I hear, sailing up and down the estuary in Alameda. But I don't think she makes it out to sea anymore.

Oh some are fond of Spanish wine,
And some are fond of French,
And some'll swallow tay and stuff
Fit only for a wench;
But I'm for right Jamaica
Till I roll beneath the bench!
(Says the old bold mate of Henry Morgan.)
—JOHN MASEFIELD, *CAPTAIN STRATTON'S FANCY*

CHAPTER 12

OVER THE YEARS, our house on Valley View Road has seen a great deal of social activity. I remember at least one costume gala, and of course many dinner parties, a great deal of music— and even a chili cookoff, where all the guests brought their own versions of chili and entered them in a contest to determine which was the best. Samples were passed around, tasted and judged; some of these were fantastically strange. I will not name the perpetrators, although I will modestly report that my version of chili was acclaimed the best. It was made with cubes of beef chuck simmered in a red New Mexico chili sauce, hot as hell, and seasoned with garlic, cumin and oregano. I'm not sure if I included beans or not.

Among our friends were Alidar "Ali" Szantho and his wife Lilly. They were Hungarian immigrants. Ali worked as an engineer, but his great passion was soccer; several times he tried to promote professional soccer leagues in the bay area and elsewhere, but these efforts came to nothing. He was of medium stature, verging on being portly, with black hair and eyes and a rather round face. He was charming and jolly, but clearly not a man with whom one would wish to trifle.

One evening we invited the Szanthos over for a "Russian" dinner party. Before the meal, Norma and Lilly sipped Bloody Marys, while Ali and I took ourselves to the buffet where caviar, blini and vodka awaited us. We took our apéritifs Russian-style, in what I then believed to be the traditional manner. The procedure is simple enough: the participant takes up a blini loaded with caviar, ingests it, and follows it with a slug of ice-cold vodka—which, it is important to emphasize, he does not simply drink but throws to the back of his throat and puts down in a single gulp. He then reaches for another caviar-laden blini and continues the procedure. So Ali and I did on that evening.

In due course Norma announced dinner. Ali and I eventually found our way to the dinner table, where Norma served a wonderfully hearty and acerbic borscht, followed by Chicken Kiev and an array of other delicacies. It was a splendid meal, enjoyed by all.

Among our other friends were Manny and Bonnie Funk. Bonnie was a cute, inoffensive little creature; Manny was slender, almost gaunt, loose-limbed, with the gesticulations, expressions and mannerisms of a natural comedian. His full name was Manfred Horman Funk. The name Funk, so Manny explained, derived from Funk's Grove in Illinois, from which, according to Manny, all the Funks in the United States originated, including the Funk of the Funk & Wagnalls publishing company. His first name resulted from his father's admiration of Baron Manfred von Richthofen, the WWI German aerial ace popularly known as "The Red Baron." Horman was Manny's mother's maiden name.

I first met Manny at the Larks Club, a lively night spot at the edge of west Oakland. Every Saturday night there was music provided by the Bearcats, a superb jazz band comprised of local musicians, with most of whom I was well acquainted. They included Bob Mielke, trombone; P. T. Stanton, cornet; Bill

Erickson, piano; Dick Oxtot, banjo; Bill Napier, clarinet; Pete Allen, bass; Don Marchant, drums. Norma and I were always in attendance, as were Manny and Bonnie. On one occasion I took down my tape recorder and recorded the performance. As I play these tapes back, I think I can hear Manny yelling "Ey, ey, ey!" and "Go! Go!" although I can't be sure. So I became acquainted with Manny; we had many jolly times thereafter.

During these years, many happy jam sessions took place at our house. The participants were various and changed from time to time, but usually K. C. Pine, who worked for the university police department, played guitar; Eubert "Red" Honoré, from New Orleans, played string bass; Manny Funk played washboard; I played cornet. We usually had Bill Erickson on piano, Bob Mielke on trombone, and others that happened to be available at the moment. I can't tell you that I was ever a high-class cornet player, but I struggled through as best I could, and despite this there was nothing that provided me more joy and euphoria than playing in a jazz band.

On one occasion, Manny Funk happened to drop into a joint in south Berkeley called the Industrial Café, and talked the proprietor into calling a band once or twice a week. I was included in this band, together with the others I have mentioned. We wanted to change the name of the place to the Sunset Café, after a famous spot in Chicago during the '20s, but the proprietor would not go for this. We played one weekend and drew a good crowd; everyone was happy, including the proprietor. The next weekend there weren't quite as many people there, and on the third weekend the attendance was even rather scanty, and the proprietor canceled the engagement. So ended my professional career as a jazz musician, although I never received anything more than a free bottle of beer for my efforts.

Manny and I had one falling-out, deriving from Manny's attempt to play the tenor saxophone and his conviction that he had succeeded in doing so. Sad to say, his best efforts yielded only halting discords which bore only the most casual relationship to the tune being played. This is a situation which, among musicians, always generates exasperation and hurt feelings.

That occasion was informal and almost impromptu. Present were only myself, Manny, Red Honoré and K. C. Pine. We started to play a tune, probably "Minnie the Mermaid," one of our favorites. Manny, instead of playing washboard—at which he was adept—began to blow into his tenor saxophone, creating what the Germans would call a *Katzenjammer*. After a painful moment or two, I halted proceedings and suggested that the music would sound better if Manny would play his washboard instead. Manny became sullen, and after a tune or two went home early.

I saw little of Manfred Horman Funk after that, which distressed me because we had had a lot of fun together. I suppose it was my fault and I should have held my tongue. A few years later I learned that he had died, possibly due to an excessive use of deleterious substances.

Another old friend, one of the few still extant, is Andrei Simić, a professor of anthropology at USC. Andrei is tall, dark, overflowing with vitality, with the merest hint of some exotic strain in his lineage. He carries himself with a jaunty swagger, and ladies turn to watch him as he saunters past. (Or at least they used to—having been blind for the last couple of decades, I can no longer attest to this firsthand.)

Andrei's father was a general in the Serbian army, and Andrei was brought up in a semi-Serbian household, which probably accounts for his area of professional expertise, which is Serbia and its culture, and that of southeastern Europe in general. He also plays Serbian gypsy music on his guitar.

Andrei and I have enjoyed many social occasions of many sorts. I recall a party at Andrei's house to which he had invited a large number of his Serbian friends, so many that the living room was crowded elbow-to-elbow. There was a small orchestra on hand playing appropriate music, to which everyone was dancing some sort of Serbian quickstep. At the center of the room was Andrei himself, his shirtsleeves rolled up, a red bandana around his head, dancing like a dervish.

🌿🌿

By the mid-1980s the house was finished. I wrote at the usual rate; then something of the old fascination for ceramics came over me.

John and I bought a steel shed, erected it; John welded a frame of angle-iron, which I lined with insulated fire-brick, and we attached a lid which was raised and lowered by means of a winch. We fired the thing with gas blowers and, all in all, I must say that the whole arrangement was nothing short of ingenious. The finished kiln could easily fire porcelain, although we never fired it that high; usually we just fired stoneware, to what is known in potters' parlance as "Cone 5," about 2,300° Fahrenheit.

We worked in white clay, red clay and black clay. As for glazes, I set out to produce them myself. In the old days the formulation of glazes was a terrible, tedious effort requiring hours of mathematical computation in order to get the balance between the constituents correct. The glaze is made up essentially of feldspar, kaolin and quartz, along with coloring oxides. I had laid in every coloring oxide available—cobalt, copper, iron, titanium, chromium.[20] Luckily, some genius in Canada had produced a computer program called *Insight*, which took all the hassle out of formulating glazes. It was such a pleasure to use this program that I could sit before my computer monitor and watch it function for hours on end, with total fascination.

But tragedy struck. I went to have my eyes examined and was diagnosed with glaucoma. A doctor hit me with some

---

20. Uranium oxide, though I didn't have any, will produce a beautiful yellow glaze; I made use of this knowledge in my early story "The Potters of Firsk."

lasers, but instead of curing the disease, scabs formed over my optic nerves and my vision quickly deteriorated. John and I sold the gear and chemicals, and nothing much of the pottery studio remains around here except an old wheel and a few plates we had made. Such was my career as a ceramicist—not very much, really, except a lot of fun.

❦❦

After my eyes went, my life became much simplified. Our travels became a thing of the past, apart from the occasional junket to a convention. I continued to write, although since longhand was obviously no longer possible, I learned to use a word processor. John modified computers with special keyboards I could feel my way around, and with what little eyesight I had left I could make out words on the monitor if they were big enough—enlarged to about ten words per screen! Eventually, however, I became totally blind and had to rely on the computer's voice synthesizer to read back what I had written. I wrote most of *Lyonesse* this way, and everything after that—*Cadwal*, *Night Lamp*, *Ports of Call* and *Lurulu*. I have no way of knowing for certain, but I may well be the only writer who bypassed the typewriter completely, going straight from longhand to computer! Still, the computer was never a perfect solution for me and writing became an increasingly laborious process as the last ray of my eyesight went glimmering. I never considered dictating my novels to tape, although this is the method I have used for this book and it has proven surprisingly adequate.

After *Lurulu* I retired from writing fiction. Finishing *Lurulu* —which I like to call my "swansong"—was like going through triage. Every now and then Jeremy, who keeps an eye on me during John's absences, gives me a poke and says, "Come on, Vance, we know there's one last Magnus Ridolph story under that tattered watchcap of yours," or, "As long as you're sitting there, you might as well plot your next mystery novel." But no, humor aside—there are no more stories in me. Only this one that I am now toward the end of telling. For one thing, I lack the inclination. That guy who wrote all that junk for so many years—he seems like another person!

I do, however, still read. The Library of Congress provides a wonderful service for the blind. They furnish a vast catalogue of books on long-playing tape and a reader on which to play them, all for free. Now that I have little to do, my existence would be a monotonous one indeed were it not for this service. Most of my waking hours are occupied listening to audiobooks. Nowadays I confine my reading mostly to murder mysteries, although occasionally to more serious works, such as anthropological treatises and histories of the ancient world. I subscribe to *Scientific American*, *Discover*, and *Popular Science*, all available in audio form, by which I try to keep more or less abreast of what is going on.

Among mystery writers, I generally prefer the British to the American—and among those, I prefer the cozies to the hard-boiled. My favorite living writer is M. C. Beaton, née Marion Chesney. I delight in her Hamish Macbeth stories; I also rather like her Agatha Raisin series, although it took me a while to warm up to the pugnacious Agatha with her "bearlike eyes" as so often described by Beaton.

I read Ruth Rendell's books if they concern Inspector Wexford; her other books, especially those written under the pseudonym Barbara Vine, are apt to be downers, and since they usually leave me in a terrible state of despondency, I avoid them. However, Rendell is without question a magnificent writer, and I admire her. The same goes for her contemporary, P. D. James.

Since we're on the subject of mystery novels, let it be known that I make no apologies for being a great admirer of Agatha Christie. It annoys me when people belittle her or take her for granted. I am also fond of Patricia Wentworth's Miss Silver books.

There are many others I could name—Patricia Moyes, Dorothy Sayers and Dorothy Simpson, Georgette Heyer— before the name-dropping grows tedious. However, I must mention three in particular, British authors, these pioneers of what is usually called "Gothic suspense" or "romantic suspense" fiction: M. M. Kaye, Mary Stewart, Victoria Holt. All three are excellent.

It has not escaped me that all the above-named writers are women. Not for me to analyze why this should be the case, I simply observe the fact. Obversely, my favorite American mystery writers happen to be men, with a couple of exceptions: Donna Leon, who writes about Commissario Guido Brunetti in Venice; and Deborah Crombie, whose books are set in the United Kingdom and seem quintessentially British although she is a native Texan. I think very highly of Lawrence Sanders—*The Anderson Tapes* is a great masterpiece—and his superb successor, Vincent Lardo, who has continued the McNally series as if Sanders were dictating to him from the grave. Bill Crider, who writes about Sheriff Dan Rhodes in Clearview, Texas, is a pleasure to read. I also include in my praise Erle Stanley Gardner, and the unfairly neglected A. B. Cunningham. Cunningham wrote in the 1940s about Sheriff Jess Roden, whose beat was the woods of rural Kentucky. And despite rumors to the contrary, I am not altogether indifferent to more recent authors. In this connection I must mention Jonathan Kellerman, whose writing I admire, and whose book *The Butcher's Theatre* I recommend to everyone. Tony Hillerman appears in my reading stack from time to time; he instills the Four Corners area of the American Southwest with an atmosphere all his own, much the way Arthur Upfield conveys a feeling for the Australian Outback. I also like Philip R. Craig's *Martha's Vineyard* books, which are highly entertaining and excellently written.

On occasion I read Ross Macdonald, Raymond Chandler and John Dickson Carr, although I have certain reservations about these authors. Chandler, for instance, while obviously a master of his craft, makes overuse of simile, to my annoyance.

Police procedurals leave me cold, although I have found that the work of the English John Creasey, writing as J. J. Marric, can be entertaining.

And I would rather have my sweet,
Though rose-leaves die of grieving,
Than do high deeds in Hungary
To pass all men's believing.
—Ezra Pound

CHAPTER 13

NEEDLESS TO SAY, I am very proud of my son John; I admire his many capabilities. I consider myself rather versatile, but John is even more so. His profession is what I shall call creative engineering; his craftsmanship is far superior to mine and he can construct or build anything he sets his mind to. At one time he played the piano with great élan, but various distractions drew him away from this pastime. He has a pilot's license, and when we owned our 45' ketch, the *Hinano*, with the south Pacific in mind, he learned celestial navigation using a sextant to take star sights and so derive latitude and longitude. This system is now of course obsolete owing to the universal use of GPS technology.

Unlike his father, John is rather handsome. He is easygoing, casual, and makes a good impression upon almost everyone with whom he comes in contact. In 1996 he married Tammy (née Tomara) Young, a charming young lady: blonde, slender, with a pleasant disposition. Norma and I came to love her as if she were our own daughter.

In due course Tammy and John produced two children: first Alison (1997), then Glen (1999). But in 2005 a great tragedy came upon us. Tammy suffered a stroke and was taken to the hospital, where daily she became less coherent and less aware, until finally she lapsed into a coma. John sat by the bed night and day and was with her when she died. I need say no more of this event.

Time passed. Alison and Glen, owing as much to good parenting as to the natural resiliency of youth, have remained sprightly and full of fun: delightful grandchildren.

One day Bill Schulz came to call. He is a mathematics professor at Northern Arizona University in Flagstaff. Bill brought along with him his two teenaged daughters: Alexia and Danae, both lively, pretty girls.

More time passed. We visited Bill and his family in Flagstaff, and on several occasions they visited us at our home in Oakland, while the girls became young ladies, and pursued Ph.D. degrees, Danae at UC Berkeley and Alexia at Harvard. Alexia has made her mark in astrophysics and Danae in molecular biology.

Bill and the two girls were often at our house. In due course, Alexia completed her Ph.D. and the next thing I knew—John and she were engaged to be married.

Early in 2008, Norma's health began to weaken seriously. John returned to Oakland, with the children, to be close to his mother during what would be her last days. She passed away quietly one evening, at home with her family.

Following her graduation, Alexia accepted a postdoctoral research position at the Institute for Advanced Study in Princeton, New Jersey. Since the fall of 2007 she, John and the children have lived there. They were joined on 6 August, 2008 by my newest grandchild, John Holbrook. He would be John Holbrook III, but John and Alexia will leave it up to him, as he grows up, whether he wishes to include the numeral after his name. I am at once tickled and flattered that they have taken to calling him—yes, you might have guessed it—Jack!

Pussycat Mew jumped over a coal,
And in her best petticoat burned a great hole;
Poor Pussy's weeping, she'll have no more milk
Until her best petticoat's mended with silk.
—Mother Goose

FINAL WORD

I HAVE BEEN counseled by my entire general staff, including my advisors, my adjutants and amanuenses—these, incidentally, are embodied in the person of Jeremy Cavaterra, who is something of a Renaissance man—to the general effect that since this is the autobiography of a writer I ought to say something about writing. Talking shop has never appealed much to me, and I have spent most of my career trying to avoid it. But Jeremy has convinced me that here it is not only suitable and fitting to break with habit, but essential. And so, I bow to the inevitable and will proceed.

My grandfather's law office was situated on the ninth floor of the Balboa building on Market Street in San Francisco, and I visited him often. In the outer office was a typewriter, and when I was eight or nine years old I sat at this typewriter and set out to write cowboy stories. I made this attempt a few times but never got much farther than two or three pages. I don't remember much about these stories, but I was here dipping my toe into what was to be my future career.

When I was about sixteen or seventeen, I was impelled to write some very silly stories describing the adventures of a group of teenagers at a seaside resort. These also have been consigned to the farthest precincts of oblivion.

I have already mentioned, in Chapter 4, that I wrote a science fiction story for my Creative English course at the university, and that the professor reviewed it in such sardonic terms that, had I been sensitive, my career would have gone glimmering. Fortunately I did not take his remarks to heart.

A few years later, some friends of mine started a science fiction society in Berkeley, which they called *The Chowder and Marching Science Fiction Society of Berkeley*. I wrote them a little story called "Seven Exits from Bocz," which they published in their magazine.

Eventually I decided to become a professional writer: I started writing stories for sale. The first of these were gadget stories, dealing with some recondite aspect of science. I sold most of them, but I don't look back on them with any pride. For a fact they were rather boring to write, and after the first few I abandoned this formula.

I then decided that my *métier* was novels, which I began to produce. The first of these I called *Clarges*, though it was published as *To Live Forever*, a title I detest.

The longer I wrote, the more I liked the results. I discovered that if I wrote to please and amuse myself, instead of editors and publishers, the books turned out better. Looking back, I am especially fond of my *Cadwal* sequence, and the latter two books of the *Durdane* set, *Emphyrio*, and more recently *Night Lamp, Ports of Call* and *Lurulu*. There are others I like as well: the so-called *Demon Princes* books, and of course the *Cugel* stories, *Rhialto the Marvellous* and the *Lyonesse* cycle.

Among the characters I've conceived, I also have my favorites: Navarth, the Mad Poet (*Demon Princes*); Baron Bodissey (*Demon Princes*), who wrote the encyclopedic tautology *Life*; also Henry Belt from "Sail 25." Among the ladies I like Wayness (*Cadwal*), and Madouc (*Lyonesse*).

My work was accomplished partly when I was at home and partly while I was traveling. At home, I always wrote longhand using four or five different fountain pens, each filled with a different color of ink. As I wrote and paused to think about something, I would begin doodling, making pretty designs on the page; then I would become absorbed with these designs, which I colored with the various inks. Most of this artwork, I regret to say, I later discarded. I think back with nostalgia about my fountain pens and colored inks.

While traveling, of course, I used only one fountain pen and plain black or blue ink. We carried with us a portable typewriter, and Norma would type my first draft, which I would edit; then she would type a second draft, to which I would make a few further emendations; at last she would type a final draft to be sent forth to my agent.

My first agent was Scott Meredith, then Kirby McCauley, and finally Ralph Vicinanza, who is still my agent, and who, so I hope, will "turn down an empty glass where I made one." Now that I think about it, there will be a lot of empty glasses turned down.

Long, long ago, when I was afflicted with wanderlust—in fact even as a boy of twelve or fourteen—I longed to drift down the Danube in a *Faltboot* from Donaueschingen to the Black Sea. I consulted maps, books, although nothing ever came of this project. There is a phrase that sticks in my memory, even while its provenance eludes me: *"Far-off places with sweet-sounding names"*. I had my own list of such names: Timbuktu, Kashmir, Bali, Tahiti, Vienna, Venice…Norma and I tried to touch in at these places over the years. The only one that we missed was Timbuktu; as outlined earlier we were close on that, at Bamako, but wisdom prevailed, and Norma and I returned home before our money ran out.

As should now be apparent, much of my work was produced while Norma, John and I inhabited some agreeable location here and there about the world. I planned this system when I was still very young, before I had written anything, and by some freak of circumstance it worked out. Of course, an equal or greater amount of my writing was done at home—I have no way of measuring this.

Early in my career I established a set of rather rigid rules as to how fiction should be written, but I find these rules difficult to formalize, or explain, or put into some sort of pattern which might instruct someone else. If I adhere to any fundamental axiom or principle in my writing, perhaps it is my belief that the function of fiction is essentially to amuse or entertain the reader. The mark of good writing, in my opinion, is that the reader is not aware that the story has been written; as he reads, the ideas and images flow into his mind as if he were living them. The utmost accolade a writer can receive is that the reader is incognizant of his presence.

In order to achieve this, the writer must put no obstacles in the reader's way. Therefore I try avoid words that he must puzzle over, or that he cannot gloss from context; and when I make up names, I shun the use of diacritical marks that he must sound out, thus halting the flow; and in general, I try to keep the sentences metrically pleasing, so that they do not obtrude upon the reader's mind. The sentences must swing. I also avoid the use of obscenity, although I notice in this present work here I've gotten a little close to the knuckle from time to time. But this is a special circumstance, and I think that I can hope for a certain degree of tolerance from my readers.

Who has been influential upon my development as a writer? Who indeed? I don't know. To name some names, I admire C. L. Moore from the old *Weird Tales* magazine. As a boy I was quite affected by the prose of Clark Ashton Smith. I revere P. G. Wodehouse. I also admire the works of Jeffery Farnol, who wrote splendid adventure books but who is today unknown except to connoisseurs of swashbuckler fiction. There are perhaps others—Edgar Rice Burroughs and his wonderful Barsoomian atmosphere; Lord Dunsany and his delicate fairylands; Baum's *Oz* books, which regrettably are of less and less interest to today's children.

❦

IN CLOSING

Now I have touched all the bases, looked right and left, up and down, examined the eleven dimensions which certain theorists say are necessary for the understanding of existence. Therefore with nothing more to report I will wave my handkerchief and say:

> *AVE ATQUE VALE!*
> *I must go down to the sea again, to the lonely sea and the sky,*
> *And all I ask is a tall ship and star to steer her by,*
> *And the wheel's kick and the wind's song and the white sail's shaking, And a gray mist on the sea's face, and a gray dawn breaking.*
> —JOHN MASEFIELD, *SEA FEVER*

ACKNOWLEDGEMENTS

As a coda to the above account, I wish to identify those persons who, in one way or another, have influenced the shape of my life and career. This list is very likely not all-inclusive, so I offer my apologies in advance to any whom I have inadvertently excluded.

My son John, his wife Alexia, and my three grandchildren.

Jeremy Cavaterra, without whose help and urging this autobiography would have gone nowhere.

Ralph Vicinanza and Vince Gerardis, my agents and friends.

Tom Doherty, my valued and even indispensable publisher.

My nephew Stephen Vance and his wife Marja.

My brother David.

Bill Schulz, my son-in-law by way of being Alexia's father, professor of mathematics, and also something of a linguist who surprises me occasionally with remarks in Basque, Celtic or even Ur-Indo-European—which of course I do not understand.

Kim Kokonnen, who provided the software which allowed me to write my last few books on the computer, thus facilitating my career.

Terry Dowling.

Andrei Simić.

David Alexander.

Paul Rhoads, who conceived the VIE.

Bob Lacovara, also instrumental in the production of the VIE.

Tim Underwood and Chuck Miller, who published many of my books.

Kevin Boudreau, who is currently assisting me in the production of my own jazz record.

Lastly, I cannot avoid mentioning people who are no longer living. I realize that this sort of thing could be carried a long way indeed; I could start acknowledging the debt of gratitude owed to Charlemagne, Alexander the Great or King Tut if I so chose, but I will not go to this extreme. I would like to mention again the name Poul Anderson, one of my dearest friends over many years, whom I admired, honored and regarded as a great gentleman.

I also wish to remember our friends Gordon, Gwen and Tony, with whom we shared so many adventures.

And I shall end with the name that began this book: my wife Norma, who worked with me throughout our married life, sharing vicissitudes and pleasures both.

PHOTO SECTION

▲ Ludwig Mathias Hoefler.

▲ Emma Hoefler.

▲ Iron House School, *circa* 1896.

◄ Sitting in front of house at 2660 Filbert Street in San Francisco, 1920.

◄ Patricia Vance, front row center, and Jack, top right, with classmates, 1928.

▲ 1938.

▲ Norma Genevieve Ingold, 1945.

▲ Jack and Edith Vance in French Gulch, 1934.

▲ In Chrysler convertible with Edith, French Gulch, CA, 1934.

▲ Sather Gate, 1938.

◀ August 24, 1946. Jerry Edelstein, Best Man, and Lois Lewis, Maid of Honor.

▲ At the beach, 1945.

▲ Norma editing *Captain Video*, 1950.

▲ *Captain Video* scripts, New York, 1950.

▲ Frank Herbert interview for Santa Rosa newspaper, 1952.

▲ Norma and Edith peeling fruit in Ibiza, 1953.

◄ Kite-flying at farmhouse near Kenwood, 1952.

Fiction Writer 'Saucer' Expert

By FRANK HERBERT

This is the way man will learn about his conquest of space: People will see a glowing dot of light in the sky. Some will say, "That's a flying saucer," or "It's the planet Venus," or "It's the inversion from a blanket of hot air."

Two groups, however, will recognize the glowing dot for what it is. These will be the scientists, and the followers of science fiction.

That's the way Jack Vance, Kenwood, a writer of science fiction, sees the glowing light which has been hovering in the sky over the Redwood Empire and which has given rise to a new rash of flying saucer stories.

HE IS ONLY semi-joking when he says that that glowing light is the atomic glare from the blast-off of man's first rocket to the moon. He has a down-to-earth scientific education from the University of California and probably agrees with his brother, Frank Vance, a sergeant with the Santa Rosa unit of the California Highway Patrol, that the planet Venus is actually the planet Venus. If enough creative imagination in him, however, to see in this phenomenon a portent of things to come.

It is his strong rooting in science which helps give his stories that elemental breath of reality essential to good fiction. This same educational background tells him that it is only a question of time until mankind controls the planet Earth and explores the rest of the solar system and, perhaps, the remainder of the universe.

A science fiction writer has to believe, Columbus-like, in the possibility of exploring the unknown. That way, he can make this possibility, expressed in his stories, believable to the reader.

THIS ELEMENT OF Mr. Vance's make-up is shown in one of his ambitions. He wants to sail around the world on a small sailboat.

"I'll do it someday, too," he said.

His wife, Norma, is a little unsure about this ambition.

"We'll face that one when we come to it," she said.

Mrs. Vance is a realistic of her husband's writing business. Mrs. Vance writes longhand. His wife transcribes the longhand copy to a typed manuscript.

The 36-year-old writer and his wife came to Sonoma County for "a little peace and quiet" in which to create the "Captain Video" television program which they are now working. "Captain Video" is a regular feature on East Coast TV.

It goes on the air one-half hour a day, 5 days a week, one story sequence running for 3 weeks.

The "Captain Video" stories have a rigid framework dictated by the show's producer, Olga Druce. In this framework, villains are normal people who are bad only temporarily and, in the end, get a chance at rehabilitation. The stories all have a moral value. There is not the slightest hint of sex overtly expressed in the stories—orders from the sponsor, Post Toasties. The pans who plays "Captain Video" has the series is completely submerged in the part, Mr. Vance said. In real life, one of his major outside activities is teaching Sunday school. On the TV screen, he supervises "Captain Video's Ranger School."

At their Kenwood ranch home, the Vances turn out these stories in groups of 3 or 4. They are a smooth-working team after 8 years of married life. They met at the University of California.

They have 9 cats—2 of their own. They are and Joe—and are boarded there by Mr. Vance's mother, Mrs. Edith Vance, Berkeley. These are really a full-time job.

The Vances turned from a where Mr. Vance regular writing to be a product of in addition to Italy.

JACK VANCE

▲ Article by Herbert.

▲ Working on Valley View house, 1955.

▲ Norma at work on house, 1955.

◀ Norma in Erfoud, Sahara, 1953.

~ 198 ~

▲ Jam session at Valley View, 1960. Bob Mielke, trombone; Judge Kroninger, tuba; Al Hall, guitar; Jack Vance, cornet.

▲ Playing in jazz orchestra at Industrial Café, Berkeley, 1961. Bill Erickson, piano; Bunky Coleman, clarinet; Pete Allen, bass; Manfred Funk, percussion; Jack Vance, cornet.

▲ John and Norma, 1962.

▲ Interior of house in Paea.

◀ John and Norma at house in Paea, Tahiti, 1964.

▲ Norma and John navigating the lagoon near Paea, Tahiti, 1964.

Frank Herbert and Poul Anderson in pontoon for houseboat, Pt. Molate, 1966.

Poul Anderson framing houseboat, with Karen, 1966.

Jack, Norma and John at John O' Groats, after journey from Land's End, 1969.

Al Hall, Jack, and Poul Anderson after salvaging sunken houseboat, 1967.

The cottage on Lough Corrib, 1969.

▲ Hard at work in front of peat fire, Lough Corrib.

▲ John navigating Lough Corrib.

▲ Lamb roast outside Madame Adriana's taverna, Corfu, 1970.

▲ Trimaran hull in driveway, Oakland, 1971.

▲ John returning from Ireland, 1973.

▲ Party at Valley View, Manny Funk and Wes Fader in foreground, 1972.

▲ Manny Funk and Andrei Simić, 1972.

▲ Graaff Reinet, 1975.

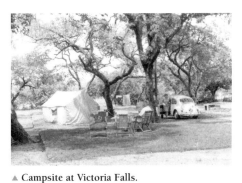

▲ Campsite at Victoria Falls.

▲ Rhodesia, 1975.

▲ Leaving Durban aboard *Karanja* bound for Karachi. Bob and Leonie Kok seeing off, 1975.

▲ Ruins in Zimbabwe, 1975.

▲ Sidetrip to Tsavo West game preserve, Kenya, 1975.

▲ Rawalpindi, Pakistan, 1975.

▲ Houseboat *Bluebird*, Nageen Lake, Kashmir.

▲ At work aboard *Bluebird*.

▲ A visit with Arthur C. Clarke at home in Ceylon, 1975.

▲ John inspecting skulls, Borneo, 1975.

▲ Longhouse, Borneo, 1975.

▲ Buying batik, Java, 1975.

◀ Valley View house nears completion, 1977.

▲ Ceramics studio, Valley View, 1983.

▲ Hinano, 1980.

▲ Breakfast with Ralph Vicinanza, 1979.

▲ Visiting Stephen and Marja Vance aboard *Twiga*, Gladstone, Australia, 1981.

▲ Dinner with Robert Palmer, Tim Underwood and friends, 1986.

▲ With Paul Rhoads at Chateau de St. Louand, Chinon, France, 1998.

▲ At the grave of Bix Beiderbecke, Davenport, Iowa, 1988.

▲ With Terry Dowling, 1997.

▲ Tammy Vance, 1998.

▲ With Ralph Vicinanza, 2008.

▲ Baby Jack, Alexia Schulz and John,
Christmas 2008

▲ Grandpa and Baby Jack, New Year's Day
2009